J. D. SALINGER

J. D. SALINGER

J. D. SALINGER
THE LAST INTERVIEW
and OTHER CONVERSATIONS

edited and with an introduction by DAVID STREITFELD

MELVILLE HOUSE
BROOKLYN · LONDON

J. D. SALINGER: THE LAST INTERVIEW
AND OTHER CONVERSATIONS

Copyright © 2016 by Melville House Publishing

Introduction copyright © 2016 by David Streitfeld

First Melville House printing: November 2016

"'The Compensations Are Few, But When They Come, If They Come, They're Very Beautiful.'" by William Maxwell © 1951 by the Book-of-the-Month Club. First published in the *Book-of-the-Month Club News* on July 1951.

"'It Was a Great Relief Telling People'" by Shirlie Blaney © 1953 by *The Claremont Daily Eagle*. First published in *The Claremont Daily Eagle* on November 13, 1953.

"J. D. Salinger Speaks About His Silence" by Lacey Fosburgh © 1974 by Lacey Fosburgh. First published in *The New York Times* on November 3, 1974.

"Ten Minutes with J. D. Salinger: How an English Teacher Survived Bad Roads, Protective Natives, Menacing Dogs and Shotgun Threats to Land an Exclusive Interview with the Legendary Hermit of Contemporary Lit I" by Greg Herriges © 1979 by Greg Herriges. First published in *Oui Magazine* in January 1979. Afterword © 2016 by Greg Herriges.

"'If You're Lonely, as Most Writers Are, Write Your Way Out of It.'" by Michael Clarkson © 1979 by Michael Clarkson. First published in the *Niagara Falls Review* on November 12, 1979. Afterword © 2016 by Michael Clarkson.

"'A Frozen Moment in Time'" by Betty Eppes © 1980 by the *Baton Rouge Sunday Advocate*. First published in the *Baton Rouge Sunday Advocate* on June 29, 1980.

"Standing In for Salinger: Confessions of J.D.'s One-Time Letter Writer" by Joanna Smith Rakoff © 2002 by Joanna Smith Rakoff. First published in *Book Magazine* in September/October 2002.

"Betraying Salinger: I Scored the Publishing Coup of the Decade: His Final Book. And Then I Blew It." by Roger Lathbury © 2010 by Roger Lathbury. First published in *New York* magazine on April 4, 2010.

Melville House Publishing
46 John Street   and
Brooklyn, NY 11201

8 Blackstock Mews
Islington
London N4 2BT

mhpbooks.com   facebook.com/mhpbooks   @melvillehouse

Library of Congress Cataloging-in-Publication Data
Names: Salinger, J. D. (Jerome David), 1919-2010. | Streitfeld, David, writer of introduction.
Title: J. D. Salinger : the last interview and other conversations / J. D. Salinger ; introduction by David Streitfeld.
Description: Brooklyn : Melville House, [2016]
Identifiers: LCCN 2016038287 (print) | LCCN 2016038331 (ebook) | ISBN 9781612195896 (pbk.) | ISBN 9781612195902 (ebook)
Subjects: LCSH: Salinger, J. D. (Jerome David), 1919-2010—Interviews. | Authors, American—20th century—Interviews.
Classification: LCC PS3537.A426 Z46 2016 (print) | LCC PS3537.A426 (ebook) | DDC 813/.54 [B] —dc23
LC record available at https://lccn.loc.gov/2016038287

Printed in the United States of America
1   3   5   7   9   10   8   6   4   2

CONTENTS

INTRODUCTION

DAVID STREITFELD

A writer's worst enemy is another writer.
—J. D. SALINGER, as quoted by
his brother-in-law Gavin,
according to Thomas Beller
in *J. D. Salinger: The Escape Artist*

J. D. Salinger was the Wizard of Oz of American letters. People journeyed for days to meet him, hoping he could cure whatever was ailing them. But Salinger's powers were limited, just like the Wizard's. He could do nothing for his fans they could not do for themselves. If you were a jerk when you ventured to his hilltop retreat in the New Hampshire village of Cornish, you were a jerk when you left town.

The legend of Salinger took root during the hopeful years of the early 1960s, when the American empire was at its zenith, progress and enlightenment were on the march, and *Time* magazine was both the celebrant and enforcer of the culture. One day, the *Time* editors set themselves a perplexing problem: What is the deal with this guy Salinger? Why does he resist the embrace of the media? What is wrong with him? It was high noon not only for the Great American Novel, that mythical beast, but also for the novelist as hero, sage, and savior, and Salinger wasn't doing his part. *Time* unleashed a vast fact-finding operation—in essence, teams of private detectives—to uncover Salinger's secrets without, the magazine assured readers, "unduly" compromising his privacy. That's what they always say.

Time's opus, "A Private World of Love and Death," appeared in the September 15, 1961, issue, available everywhere for twenty-five cents. The tone is set in the first paragraph, just after the inevitable quote from *The Catcher in the Rye* about Holden wanting to build a cabin in the woods where he would pretend to be "one of those deaf-mutes" so "I wouldn't have to have any goddam stupid useless conversations with anybody." The magazine then describes a hilltop house in the woods where the recluse lives. "Not long ago," *Time* recounts, "when he and his family were away, a couple of neighbors could stand it no longer, put on dungarees and climbed over the 6½-ft. fence to take a look around."

Stop right there. What is the "it" that these neighbors could not stand, that drove presumably law-abiding folks to unlawful entry? Was it not knowing the details of a life they had no right to know? Was it Salinger's crankiness, his disdain? *Time* does not say, but "it" proved a powerful force for at least forty years, motivating nosy neighbors, trashy as

well as respectable reporters, devout fans, and the merely curious. The number who made the pilgrimage to the hilltop was
easily in the hundreds if not thousands, and the reports they
brought back of their success or, more often, failure helped
set the pattern for modern tabloid culture, where the media's,
and perhaps even the public's, eagerness to know is pitted
against the celebrity's right not to be known. Even if the even-
tual winner was never in doubt, if Salinger was reduced to
posting signs that demanded, or maybe begged, "No hunting,
trapping, fishing, or trespassing of ANY kind," the battle, at
least for a time, was surprisingly well matched.

The *Time* archives, eventually shared with researchers,
reveal relentless pursuit. "We have found a lead that may
finally open Mr. Salinger's closet of little girls," a telex from
one correspondent proclaims. The real-life model for Sybil,
the young girl befriended by Seymour in "A Perfect Day
for Bananafish"—widely considered one of the most flaw-
less if supremely enigmatic short stories ever written—is
tracked down. She proves wonderfully reluctant. "J. tried
to be aloof . . ." another correspondent informs the editors.
"Didn't remember where she had met Salinger or what he was
like. Well, did she deny that, as a child, she had known him
in Florida? She puffed on her cigarette a moment, as if debat-
ing over which plea to enter: 'Yes,' she said carefully, 'I think
I do deny it.'"

Disappointments like these provoked an icy rage in the
Time editors. "One source of bogus information is the author
himself," the magazine noted, pointing out that in the jacket
blurb for *Franny and Zooey*, which Salinger wrote himself,
"he says with coy fraudulence that 'I live in Westport with my

dog.' The dark facts are that he has not lived in Westport or had a dog for years."

A few weeks later, another part of the *Time* empire, *Life* magazine, published its own Why-is-Salinger-hiding? story. It was illustrated with a big photo of the writer's fence. At the bottom, in the little gap between fence and ground, lurked what *Life* boldly identified as "the family dog." Ian Hamilton, who wrote the first biography of Salinger twenty-five years later, pointed out the discrepancy and commented that, if nothing else, Salinger should have found grim satisfaction in the fact that America's two most powerful newsmagazines could not manage to agree on whether he owned a dog.

Hamilton himself was bested by the recluse. *J. D. Salinger: A Writing Life* was cautious and brief, but the biographer made the mistake of quoting from a number of Salinger's lively letters, which were protected by copyright. Salinger chased Hamilton all the way up to the Supreme Court, which was not surprising, and won, which was. But Salinger's victory, as usual, was purchased at high cost. The more he tried to defend himself, the more people bugged him, with predictable results: they made up interviews, sold his letters, dished to journalists, pirated his stories. As he once wrote to a woman he was wooing, "To be a success is to be a failure."

The notion that if you fight too much for your privacy you'll lose your privacy was a lesson for artists like Don De-Lillo. His 1991 novel *Mao II* was inspired by a photo on the cover of the *New York Post* that showed a cadaverous Salinger literally lashing out at two photographers who stalked him in a parking lot. The headline: "Catcher caught."

"When a writer doesn't show his face, he becomes a local

symptom of God's famous reluctance to appear," DeLillo observed. He surrendered enough of himself to journalists so they left him alone when he went out for groceries.

Salinger's only weapon against this perpetual onslaught was that he could see through people. Approach him as an admirer—and really mean it—and he might talk to you or reply to your earnest letter, and that brief encounter could change your life. Approach him cynically, as a writer in search of a scoop, and you would be showered with bad karma, possibly forever, although Salinger knew he would suffer too. He anticipated his fate, as novelists often do.

"I know I am known as a strange, aloof kind of person," he said. "I pay for this attitude."

The pieces in this book are time capsules. Anyone seeking out Salinger between 1950 and around 1985 was dealing with very limited information, and some of that inevitably turned out to be myth or at least misleading. These accounts are printed as they were originally published, aside from a few glaring grammatical or typographical errors. Joanna Smith Rakoff and Roger Lathbury, who wrote the last two articles, both talked to Salinger, but their tales could not even be loosely described as interviews. They are codas, intimate reports from those who gained access to Fortress Salinger by other means.

There's an old joke that the collected J. D. Salinger interviews could be titled *Get Off My Lawn*. That's because he never did interviews. So people always said. Even Salinger said it. Ian Hamilton asked for an interview at the beginning

of his biography, knowing full well he wasn't going to get it
but hardly expecting Salinger's blistering response:

> Speaking (as you may have gathered) from rather
> unspeakably bitter experience, I suppose I can't
> put you or Random House off, if the lot of you are
> determined to have your way, but I do feel I must
> tell you, for what very little it may be worth, that I
> think I've borne all the exploitation and loss of pri-
> vacy I can possibly bear in a single lifetime.

It sounds like melodrama, or possibly a crazy person, but
Salinger was speaking plainly. The public part of his deposition
in his lawsuit is printed here in full for the first time anywhere.
(The second part was sealed.) It includes this revealing snippet:

> **CALLAGY**: Have other people in the last twenty-five
> years asked you for an interview?
>
> **SALINGER**: Oh, yes.
>
> **CALLAGY**: Have you ever granted an interview to
> anyone?
>
> **SALINGER**: Knowledgeably? No.
>
> **CALLAGY**: Have you ever granted an interview un-
> knowledgeably to anyone?
>
> **SALINGER**: Apparently, yes.

I would like to imagine Salinger smiling ruefully as he said that, but it's doubtful. In any case, he still wasn't quite accurate. He talked to his friend William Maxwell for the *Book-of-the-Month-Club News* when *Catcher* was published in 1951, although to call it an interview is stretching it a bit. Only once is Salinger quoted directly.

Two years later, he chatted with sixteen-year-old Shirlie Blaney, although the circumstances are in dispute, as they often are with Salinger. According to what Blaney—always described as attractive, perky, blonde—later told *Life* magazine, she used to go to parties at Salinger's house with other teens. They'd listen to records, drink Cokes, and eat potato chips. Salinger was quiet, soaking it in. Was he plotting his next novel or just grooving on the moment? Blaney wasn't sure.

Blaney was a student journalist, one of a group that wrote a monthly page for the local paper, the *Claremont Daily Eagle*. But there wasn't much news in rural New Hampshire, so when she saw Jerry Salinger on the street she asked for "something I can write about." Sure, he said. Blaney and a friend took Salinger into the soda fountain, peppered him with questions, and wrote a piece that the *Daily Eagle* liked so much that it was elevated to the editorial page. After Salinger read it, he never talked to Blaney again or invited the teenagers back. He put up the big fence and got married.

That was how Blaney told the story. Salinger might have been bothered by the piece's numerous errors, the fact that it called him "foreign-looking" (code for "Jew"), or most likely its mere existence. His feelings were perhaps sharpened by the fact that—according to Shane Salerno and David Shields's authoritative *Salinger* (2013)—he and Blaney were dating.

Salinger was in his early thirties. Parents these days would call the cops.

The betrayal lingered. In 1978, when the editor of the Windsor High student newspaper wanted to reprint the piece and wrote Salinger for permission, he got back a note calling the interview "a rank piece of deception, manipulation, exploitation, and misrepresentation." (Forget about the fact that Salinger did not own the copyright and could not in fact grant permission.) Blaney got married and moved away, and even Salerno and Shields, who tried to interview everyone in the Salinger universe, did not mange to talk to her.

It wasn't the last time Salinger fell for a dame. As with many men of that era, his weakness was women, the younger the better. Betty Eppes grew up poor in the rural South, never graduated from high school, and had three children during an early marriage, but she had enough ambition and talent to refashion herself as an ace tennis player, then a tennis columnist, and finally a feature writer for the *Baton Rouge Sunday Advocate*. Eppes was forty but looked much younger when she hit on the notion of interviewing Salinger in 1980. She did not go seeking enlightenment like previous pilgrims. Fame was the lure. The result was disastrous for all concerned.

Eppes's rarely seen original article, reprinted in this volume, is a credible piece of writing. Like most journalism of the pre-Internet era, it does not reveal what happened behind the scenes, which is that Eppes tricked Salinger into meeting her. She wrote him a note saying she was an aspiring novelist who thought writing was "so hard" and wanted to talk to him about it. She added that she would be driving a sky-blue Pinto and had green eyes and red-gold hair.

She didn't mention her newspaper or that she would be taping him.

Salinger showed up on time. "I came here one writer to another," he said, which is why he was willing to answer questions about writing but not anything else. Eppes's real troubles began when George Plimpton, the editor of *The Paris Review* and a man who delighted in mischief, got hold of her article and transformed it. Plimpton was under the impression that Eppes was in her twenties, and he recast the piece into a first-person article that emphasized her girlishness:

> I knew that Salinger would be spooked by the sight of a tape recorder, but also that it would be crazy to try to talk to him scribbling away in his face. So I thought *Hell*, I'll stuff the tape recorder down my blouse under my long-sleeved sweater. It was difficult to do without looking like I had some kind of deformity. I thought, Jeez—I wouldn't want J. D. Salinger to think I've got a square boob. So I finally shoveled the tape recorder down the sleeve of my blouse right under my armpit where I could hold it in against my body with my arm. I thought, if I just keep my elbow in, everything will be cool.

The piece, "What I Did Last Summer," appeared in the Summer 1981 issue of *The Paris Review*. Plimpton trumpeted it as the equivalent of a full-fledged *Paris Review* interview with Salinger, the writer's final word to succeeding generations. This new account circulated much more widely than

the newspaper story. As usual, the novelist who didn't want
to talk was blamed for talking. "One could argue he came because he knew Eppes would write about the meeting, something that would generate publicity for him," biographer Paul
Alexander wrote.

Some people who read it took Salinger's side. "One of
the worst examples of journalism ethics I have ever encountered," Warren Eyster, an assistant professor of English at
Louisiana State, wrote in Eppes's own newspaper. "Salinger
owes her a punch in the nose *and* a lawsuit."

According to Eppes, the first of these very nearly happened. Toward the end of *The Paris Review* piece, a local man
sees Salinger talking to Eppes and decides to have his own
conversation with the writer. He even tries to shake Salinger's
hand. Salinger got visibly upset, then circled back to Eppes
and blamed her.

Many years later, Eppes complained that "Salinger's
tongue lashing was unseemly to my mind," and then dropped
a revelation: "But it was nothing compared to the verbal
storm he unleashed after discovering I'd taped our conversation. Posturing, and using language he clearly expected to
intimidate me, he demanded I hand the tape over to him.
Salinger seemed truly shocked when I refused." None of that
is in the *Paris Review* piece.

Eppes stopped writing for the *Advocate* in 1990. She
moved to Costa Rica and then moved back when a love affair
went bad. She wrote on her blog that she hoped when her
former partner "gets back to his native country (one famous
for its apples), that every apple he eats will create a fire pit in
his gut of such heat it will make Dante's inferno look like the

friendly fire of a tea-light candle." She seems to wish much the same on Plimpton for tarting up her story.

In cryptic blog comments, Eppes recast her encounter with Salinger yet again, this time saying it led to a relationship that was much longer and deeper than she had intimated. "After my article was published, Salinger called me, as he frequently did," she wrote. She maintains she saw him again as well: "Salinger proved each time we met that he was a complex, difficult man." Or maybe he just really wanted the tape: "He asked me to give control over it to him many times but I refused, which strained our acquaintanceship but did not destroy it."

How believable is all of this? "One day, I will tell all," Eppes said. "But not just yet." Now in her late seventies, she has not updated her blog for years and did not respond to my emails. Like Blaney, she has followed Salinger into silence. Perhaps that is a fitting fate for the woman who did so much to reinforce Salinger's own desire for privacy. Six months after Eppes's interview, Mark David Chapman shot John Lennon, citing *Catcher* as his "statement." From that point on, no one who showed up unannounced on Salinger's doorstep had a prayer, no matter how good-looking she was.

Too bad. He seems in many ways to have been a sweet man—touchy as hell, of course, but that's not the worst sin in a writer, nor the most uncommon. Every hack who wants to score cheap points off Salinger quotes the passage in *Catcher* about how great it would be to call up an author after reading his book—and then points out that Salinger ordered his literary agents to destroy all fan mail instead of forwarding it. But this is a position that Salinger was forced into. Even as he withdrew from publishing, he kept reading the letters of hopeful young people, and sometimes even responding.

He wrote a lovely letter to one high school senior, for instance, declining her request to come talk at her graduation but including "a private little graduation speech" especially for her. He offered his hope that she would have "a terrific, lovely, thoughtful, useful, happy time doing whatever she does next after high school," adding "all [your] chances seem to me really first class." He also said, in a very Salinger-ish comment, that he found the idea of writers declaiming to graduating classes highly objectionable: "In any really thoughtful list of blights and scourges of our time, talking writers, surely, ought to be somewhere up very close to the top."

It's time for me to enter the story. Anyone hitting his teenage years on the East Coast during the 1970s was exposed to Salinger. It was a rite of passage, like losing your virginity, taking your first hit of marijuana, or learning to drive. Probably you were assigned *Catcher* in eleventh-grade English, like I was, and carried that shiny maroon Bantam paperback around for weeks, looking for clues. It was a depressing decade, and depressed Holden offered some solace by being even more of a screw-up than any of his readers.

After writing an unpublished novel or two composed in deepest Salingerese, I wound up at *The Washington Post*. Salinger was part of the backdrop of contemporary letters and life. My friend Allan Milkerit, a book scout of rare skill, once acquired from God knows where a contract that Salinger had signed to pay for a cruise. Salinger put his phone number on it, and I promptly wrote it down, carrying it in my wallet for years. *If found unconscious, please call J. D. Salinger.*

I met William Maxwell, a longtime fiction editor of *The New Yorker*, partly because I was curious about Salinger. When Salinger finished writing *Catcher*, he drove to Maxwell's house in the country and over the course of a long afternoon and evening read it aloud to the editor and his wife, Emily. I was once visiting Maxwell in his Manhattan apartment, one of those spacious spaces that no one aside from hedge-fund managers can now afford. I was standing near the bookshelves, idly gazing, when my left arm started to rise of its own volition. It had found a copy of *Catcher*, with the photo of Salinger on the back indicating a first edition. It was inscribed, "To Bill—I couldn't have done it without you, Love, Jerry," or words to that effect. I put the book back on the shelf, where it was casually nestled between a volume of Tolstoy and one of Turgenev. I've sometimes wondered what happened to it after Maxwell's death. Thrown out in the trash? Passed on to relatives who stuck it in a box in the attic? This would have been the ultimate collector's copy, worth six figures, no questions asked.

Maxwell was as cagey about Salinger as he was about many things, partly because he knew Salinger didn't like to be talked about, but he would tell this story: A *New Yorker* copy editor had once said a Salinger story needed a comma, and Maxwell agreed. Since the story was going to press, there was no time to reach Salinger. When Salinger saw the story in print, he was not mad but something worse: he was sad. Maxwell said he learned a few lessons from that.

Perhaps Salinger was waiting for someone to come along—an amateur—who had the same hyper-attention to detail, and the same reverence for the work, that the author himself did. That person finally emerged in 1996 in Roger Lathbury, an English professor at George Mason University, who recounts his tale in this volume. Lathbury, who ran a small press, wanted to reprint Salinger's last published story, "Hapworth 16, 1924," a 26,000-word story from 1965 told by seven-year-old Seymour Glass, and Salinger agreed to let him do it. For a guy who did not permit any stories to be reprinted in anthologies, who shut down a site on the nascent Web that let readers start off the day with a random *Catcher* quote, and who refused to collect his early work even after it had been pirated, the decision to add a fifth book to the canonical four was startling.

Lathbury tried to keep things quiet, but he was too honest to dissemble. A story appeared in the November 15, 1996, issue of the *Washington Business Journal*, which took the local-press-makes-good angle. News traveled slower back then, and the gulf separating the local business sheet from any media that would have cared about its Salinger scoop was immense. If publication had remained January 1, 1997—Salinger's seventy-eighth birthday—it would not have mattered. But the date slipped, as these things do.

By then I was the publishing correspondent at the *Post*, a job that let me live and breathe literature. I tried to follow up on the *Journal* scoop, writing a letter to Salinger and calling his agent. Neither effort yielded any result. I printed an item in my book column on January 12 about the impending publication, just a few sentences. My editors realized this was big news. I called Lathbury and wrote a full article on January 17. That did it. Media around the world followed suit. A few weeks later, Michiko Kakutani delivered the coup de grâce in *The New York Times*, reviewing "Hapworth" as if it were a published book. She called it "a sour, implausible and, sad to say, completely charmless story." Publication was never officially canceled. It simply never happened.

I blame myself, not Kakutani. So did the *Post*, in a story about Lathbury published after Salinger's death in 2010. My article, it said, "reached Salinger and torpedoed the deal."

I think I failed the test of being pure enough. When I called Lathbury he said he had read "Hapworth" when it came out in 1965.

"I think it's true," he said.

True?

"The story. What it says. The main character is right."

No wonder Salinger gave him the go-ahead. "Hapworth" separates the run-of-the-mill Salinger fan from the true devotee. Personally, I could not admire the story, or even make my way through it. I would get to the end of one sentence and realize I had no memory of what I had read and would start over:

I tell you now, this very moment, to please tuck away someplace utterly unmelancholy in your memory against a rainy day, that until the hour we finish our lives there will always be innumerable chaps who get very seething, and thoroughly inimical even when they see our bare faces alone coming over the horizon. Mark you, I am saying our faces alone, independent of our peculiar and

often offensive personalities! There would be a fairly
humorous side to the matter if I had not watched it
happen with sickening dismay too many hundred
times in my brief years. I am hoping, however, that
as we continue to improve and refine our characters
by leaps and bounds, striving each day to reduce
general snottiness, surface conceits, and too damn
much emotion, coupled with several other quali-
ties quite rotten to the core, we will antagonize and
inspire less murder, on sight or repute alone, in the
hearts of fellow human beings.

If I had heard the music here, maybe my hand would have
been stayed, Lathbury's project would have remained secret,
and the book would have been published. I took my failure as
a signal to get out. I soon gave up writing about literature and
moved to the West Coast, yet another example of Salinger's
ability to reshape lives.

"All writers," Salinger once wrote in a biographical note, "go
to their graves half–Oliver Twist and half–Mary, Mary Quite
Contrary." I take this to mean they don't do what you think
they should do, sometimes even doing things against their
own self-interest, but that they are also yearning for more
and more and more, no matter what their ego or diffidence
or success. The writer on top of the bestseller list wants the
Pulitzer Prize. The Nobel winner wants his books on every
street corner.

By the end of his life, Salinger was as much a relic as a manual typewriter. Literary writers were no longer generating the sort of out-of-control emotions that he effortlessly provoked for decades. No one is trying to stalk last year's acclaimed new novelist. For one thing, if you tune to the right Internet channel, writers are broadcasting continuously, letting us know via Twitter their opinions on the latest outrage and on Facebook how they discovered a great recipe for meatloaf. It's hard to long for someone who never goes away.

Popular culture, on the other hand, still breeds obsessive fans. Far from being outcasts, they are now vital components of the system. Annie Wilkes, the crazy admirer in Stephen King's *Misery* who rescues her favorite novelist from a car crash and keeps him captive so he can produce the work she wants, has evolved from a figure of horror to a role model. Fans rule.

Salinger would have loathed this development. He didn't even allow movies to be made from his work (aside from one early misbegotten exception), much less permit fan fiction to get Holden laid or end up with the deaf-mutes. It was a purist attitude—the creator as God—and these days a very lonely one.

And yet. If Salinger was both contrarian and eager for more, his demanding Oliver side ended up more than fulfilled. The writer's death in 2010 was the biggest literary event of the era, at least until the discovery of Harper Lee's lost draft of *To Kill a Mockingbird* provoked a frenzy in 2015.

In both cases, gifted writers had become legends by not writing. For some spectators, Salinger's vanishing act trumped the published work. "Silence, it turns out, was Salinger's most brilliant career move and most interesting creation," critic Stephen Kessler wrote, adding that the writer "succeeded, through his very invisibility, in making himself an almost monumental literary figure."

Here's one way to appreciate how Salinger took himself out of the narrative: when National Public Radio went looking for a snippet of Salinger's voice to play on the air after his death, it couldn't find one.

Now that there's no point in going to the hilltop, all that remains is the work. You can't hear his real voice, but the literary voice is instantly recognizable and still compelling:

> When you're dead they really fix you up. I hope to hell when I do die somebody has sense enough to just dump me in the river or something. Anything except sticking me in a goddamned cemetery. People coming and putting a bunch of flowers on your stomach on Sunday, and all that crap. Who wants flowers when you're dead? Nobody.

He got his wish. Find A Grave, the helpful website that lets you track down the resting place of loved ones, lists Salinger under "BURIAL: UNKNOWN."

"THE COMPENSATIONS ARE FEW, BUT WHEN THEY COME, IF THEY COME, THEY'RE VERY BEAUTIFUL."

INTERVIEW BY WILLIAM MAXWELL
BOOK-OF-THE-MONTH CLUB NEWS
JULY 1951

Jerome David Salinger was born in New York City on January 1, 1919. So far as the present population is concerned, there is a cleavage between those who have come to the city as adults and those who were born and raised there, for a New York childhood is a special experience. For one thing, the landmarks have a very different connotation. As a boy Jerry Salinger played on the steps of public buildings that a nonnative would recognize immediately and that he never knew the names of. He rode his bicycle in Central Park. He fell into the Lagoon. Those almost apotheosized department stores, Macy's and Gimbel's, still mean to him the toy department at Christmas. Park Avenue means taking a cab to Grand Central at the beginning of vacation.

Since there is no positive evidence to the contrary, it is reasonable to assume that people who have any kind of artistic talent are born with it. Something is nevertheless required to set talent in operation. With a writer I think what is required is a situation, something that is more than he can hope to handle. At the age of fifteen, Salinger was sent to military school, which he not very surprisingly detested. At night in bed, under the covers, with the aid of a flashlight, he began writing stories. He has been writing ever since, writing constantly, and often in places as inconvenient as a totally dark, cold, school dormitory.

He was graduated from military school and went to college, in a manner of speaking—to several colleges; but he didn't let the curriculum interfere with his self-imposed study of professional writers. Sometimes the curriculum and his plans coincided, and he was able to take a course in writing. The other students went straight for the large themes: life and death. Salinger's choice of subject matter was always unambitious, his approach to it that of a craftsman.

In the midst of his college period, his father sent him to Europe for a year to learn German and to write ads for a firm that exported Polish hams. It was a happy year. He lived in Vienna, with an Austrian family, and learned some German and a good deal about people, if not about the exporting business. Eventually he got to Poland and for a brief while went out with a man at four o'clock in the morning and bought and sold pigs. Though he hated it, there is no experience, agreeable or otherwise, that isn't valuable to a writer of fiction. He wrote and sent what he wrote to magazines in America—and learned, as well as this ever can be learned, how not to mind when the manuscripts came back to him.

During the first part of his army service he corrected papers in a ground school for aviation cadets by day; and at night, every night, he wrote. Later he wrote publicity releases for Air Service Command in Dayton, Ohio, and used his three-day passes to go to a hotel and write stories. At the end of 1943 he was transferred to the Counter-Intelligence Corps. He landed in France on D-Day with the 4th Division, and remained with it, as one of two special agents responsible for the security of the 12th Regiment, for the rest of the war, through five campaigns.

He is now living in a rented house in Westport, Connecticut, with, for company and distraction, a Schnauzer named Benny, who, he says, is terribly anxious to please and always has been. Salinger has published, all told, about thirty stories. How completely unlike anybody else's stories they are, and also something of their essential quality, three of the titles convey: "A Perfect Day for Bananafish," "Just Before the War with the Eskimos," and "For Esme—With Love and Squalor."

The Catcher in the Rye was originally a novelette ninety pages long. This version was finished in 1946, and a publisher was willing to publish it, but the author, dissatisfied, decided to do it over again. The result is a full-length book, much richer, deeper, more subjective and more searching. It means little or nothing to say that a novelist writes like Flaubert, since Flaubert invented the modern novel with *Madame Bovary*, and it is probably impossible not to write like him in one way or another, but it means a great deal to say that a novelist *works* like Flaubert (which Salinger does), with infinite labor, infinite patience, and infinite thought for the technical aspects of what he is writing, none of which must show in the final draft. Such writers go straight to heaven when they die, and their books are not forgotten.

"A year or so ago," he says, "I was asked to speak to a short-story class at Sarah Lawrence College. I went, and I enjoyed the day, but it isn't something I'd ever want to do again. I got very oracular and literary. I found myself labeling all the writers I respect. (Thomas Mann, in an introduction he wrote for *The Castle*, called Kafka a 'religious humorist.' I'll never forgive him for it.) A writer, when he's asked to discuss his craft, ought to get up and call out in a loud voice just the *names* of the writers he *loves*. I love Kafka, Flaubert, Tolstoy, Chekhov, Dostoyevsky, Proust, O'Casey, Rilke, Lorca, Keats, Rimbaud, Burns, E. Bronte, Jane Austen, Henry James, Blake, Coleridge. I won't name any living writers. I don't think it's right. I think writing is a hard life. But it's brought me enough happiness that I don't think I'd ever deliberately dissuade anybody (if he had talent) from taking it up. The compensations are few, but when they come, if they come, they're very beautiful."

"IT WAS A GREAT RELIEF TELLING PEOPLE"

INTERVIEW BY SHIRLIE BLANEY
THE CLAREMONT DAILY EAGLE
NOVEMBER 13, 1953

During the preparation of the recent student edition of the Daily Eagle, *Miss Shirlie Blaney of the class of 1954 at Windsor High School spied Jerome David Salinger, author of the bestseller* Catcher in the Rye, *in a Windsor restaurant. Mr. Salinger, who recently bought a home in Cornish, obliged the reporter with the following interview.*

An author of many articles and a few stories, including *Catcher in the Rye*, was interviewed and provided us with an interesting life story.

A very good friend of all the high school students, Mr. Salinger has many older friends as well, although he has been coming here only a few years. He keeps very much to himself, wanting only to be left alone to write. He is a tall and foreign-looking man of 34, with a pleasing personality.

Jerome David Salinger was born January 1, 1919, in New York. He went to public grammar schools, while his high school years were spent at Valley Forge Military Academy in Pennsylvania. During this time he was writing. His college

education included New York University, where he studied
for two years.

With his father, he went to Poland to learn the ham shipping business. He didn't care for this, but he accomplished
something by learning the German language.

Later he was in Vienna for ten months, but came back
and went to Ursinus College. Due to lack of interest, he left
at mid-years and went to Columbia University. All this time
he was still writing.

Mr. Salinger's first story was published at the age of
21. He wrote for two years for the *Saturday Evening Post*,
Esquire, *Mademoiselle*, and many more. He later worked on
the liner *Kungsholm* in the West Indies, as an entertainer.
He was still writing for magazines and college publications.
At the age of 23, he was drafted. He spent two years in the
Army, which he disliked because he wanted all of his time
to write.

He started working on *Catcher in the Rye*, a novel, in 1941
and finished it in the summer of 1951. It was a Book-of-the-
Month Club selection for the month, and later came out as a
pocket book.

The book is a study of a troubled adolescent boy. When
asked if it was in any way autobiographical, Mr. Salinger said:
"Sort of, I was much relieved when I finished it. My boyhood
was very much the same as that of the boy in the book, and it
was a great relief telling people about it."

About two years ago he decided to come to New England. He came through this section. He liked it so much that
he bought his present home in Cornish.

His plans for the future include going to Europe and

Indonesia. He will go first to London, perhaps to make a movie.

One of his books, *Uncle Wiggley in Connecticut*, has been made into a movie, *My Foolish Heart.*

About 75 percent of his stories are about people under 21 and 40 per cent of those about youngsters under 12.

His second book was a collection of nine stories. They first appeared in *The New Yorker.*

J. D. SALINGER SPEAKS ABOUT HIS SILENCE

INTERVIEW BY LACEY FOSBURGH
THE NEW YORK TIMES
NOVEMBER 3, 1974

Goaded by publication of unauthorized editions of his early, previously uncollected works, the reclusive author J. D. Salinger broke a public silence of more than 20 years last week, issuing a denunciation and revealing he is hard at work on writings that may never be published in his lifetime.

Speaking by telephone from Cornish, N.H., where he makes his home, the 55-year-old author, whose most recent published work, *Raise High the Roof Beam, Carpenters* and *Seymour: An Introduction*, appeared in 1963, said: "There is a marvelous peace in not publishing. It's peaceful. Still. Publishing is a terrible invasion of my privacy. I like to write. I love to write. But I write just for myself and my own pleasure."

For nearly half an hour after saying he intended to talk "only for a minute," the author, who achieved literary fame and cultish devotion enhanced by his inaccessibility following publication of *The Catcher in the Rye* in 1951, spoke of his work, his obsession with privacy, and his uncertain thoughts about publication.

The interview with Mr. Salinger, who was at times warm and charming, at times wary and skittish, is believed to be his first since 1953, when he granted one to a 16-year-old representative of the high school newspaper in Cornish.

What prompted Mr. Salinger to speak now on what he said was a cold, rainy, windswept night in Cornish was what he regards as the latest and most severe of all invasions of his private world: the publication of *The Complete Uncollected Short Stories of J. D. Salinger*, volumes 1 and 2.

During the last two months, about 25,000 copies of these books, priced at $3 to $5 for each volume, have been sold—first here in San Francisco, then in New York, Chicago, and elsewhere, according to Mr. Salinger, his lawyers, and book dealers around the country.

"Some stories, my property, have been stolen," Mr. Salinger said. "Someone's appropriated them. It's an illicit act. It's unfair. Suppose you had a coat you liked and somebody went into your closet and stole it. That's how I feel."

Mr. Salinger wrote the stories, including two about Holden Caulfield, the pained, sensitive hero of *The Catcher in the Rye*, between 1940 and 1948 for magazines like *The Saturday Evening Post*, *Collier's*, and *Esquire*.

Prefiguring his later writing, they concern themselves with lonely young soldiers and boys who eat egg yolks, girls with "lovely, awkward" smiles, and children who never get letters.

"They're selling like hotcakes," said one San Francisco book dealer. "Everybody wants one."

While *The Catcher in the Rye* still sells at the rate of 250,000 copies a year, the contents of the unauthorized paperback books have been available heretofore only in the magazine files of large libraries.

"I wrote them a long time ago," Mr. Salinger said of the stories, "and I never had any intention of publishing them. I wanted them to die a perfectly natural death.

"I'm not trying to hide the gaucheries of my youth. I just don't think they're worthy of publishing."

Since last April, copies of *The Complete Uncollected Short Stories of J. D. Salinger*, volumes 1 and 2, have reportedly been peddled in person to bookstores at $1.50 each by men who always call themselves John Greenberg and say they come from Berkeley, Calif. Their descriptions have varied from city to city.

One such peddler told Andreas Brown, manager of the Gotham Book Mart in New York City, that he and his associates did not expect to get in trouble for their unauthorized enterprise because, as Mr. Brown related, "they could always negotiate with Salinger's lawyers and promise not to do it any more."

Mr. Brown, who described the young man as "a hippie, intellectual type, a typical Berkeley student," said, "I asked him why they were doing it, and he said he was a fan of Salinger's and thought these stories should be available to the public.

"I asked him what he thought Salinger would feel, and he said, 'We thought if we made the books attractive enough he wouldn't mind.'"

Gotham refused to sell the books and alerted Mr. Salinger to the unauthorized publications.

"It's irritating," said Mr. Salinger, who said he still owns the copyright on the stories. "It's really very irritating. I'm very upset about it."

According to Neil L. Shapiro, one of the author's lawyers here, the publication or sale of the stories without Mr. Salinger's authorization violates federal copyright laws.

A civil suit in Mr. Salinger's name was filed last month in the Federal District Court here against "John Greenberg" and 17 major local bookstores, including Brentano's, alleging violation of the copyright laws.

The author is seeking a minimum of $250,000 in punitive damages and injunctive relief.

The stores have since been enjoined from all further sales of the unauthorized books, and, according to Mr. Shapiro, they still face possible damage payments ranging from $4,500 to $90,000 for each book sold. Additional legal action, he said, was being planned against bookstores elsewhere.

The mysterious publisher and his associates remain at large.

"It's amazing some sort of law and order agency can't do something about this," Mr. Salinger said. "Why, if a dirty old mattress is stolen from your attic, they'll find it. But they're not even looking for this man."

Discussing his opposition to republication of his early works, Mr. Salinger said they were the fruit of a time when he was first beginning to commit himself to being a writer. He spoke of writing feverishly, of being "intent on placing [his works] in magazines."

Suddenly he interrupted himself.

"This doesn't have anything to do with this man Greenberg," he said. "I'm still trying to protect what privacy I have left."

Over the years many newspapers and national magazines have sent their representatives to his farmhouse in Cornish, but the author would turn and walk away if approached on the street and was reported to abandon friends if they discussed him with reporters. There have been articles reporting on his mailbox, his shopping, and his reclusive life, but not interviews.

But last week, he responded to a request for an interview transmitted to him earlier in the day by Dorothy Olding, his New York literary agent.

Did he expect to publish another work soon?

There was a pause.

"I really don't know how soon," he said. There was another pause, and then Mr. Salinger began to talk rapidly about how much he was writing, long hours, every day, and he said he was under contract to no one for another book.

"I don't necessarily intend to publish posthumously," he said, "but I do like to write for myself.

"I pay for this kind of attitude. I'm known as a strange, aloof kind of man. But all I'm doing is trying to protect myself and my work.

"I just want all this to stop. It's intrusive. I've survived a lot of things," he said in what was to be the end of the conversation, "and I'll probably survive this."

TEN MINUTES WITH J. D. SALINGER

HOW AN ENGLISH TEACHER SURVIVED BAD ROADS, PROTECTIVE NATIVES, MENACING DOGS AND SHOTGUN THREATS TO LAND AN EXCLUSIVE INTERVIEW WITH THE LEGENDARY HERMIT OF CONTEMPORARY LIT I

INTERVIEW BY GREG HERRIGES
OUI MAGAZINE
JANUARY 1979

Amid the drone of the overhead projector's fan and the monotone of the teacher's voice, there was an oasis in the high school English classes of the Fifties and the early Sixties. Against a dismal, gray background of subordinate clauses and dangling participles, one really relevant and gloriously luminous piece of fiction emerged: *The Catcher in the Rye*. It was what saved the generation that reached puberty after Hiroshima and before The Beatles. The book's immortal protagonist, Holden Caulfield, and his creator, J. D. Salinger, became fantasy protectors, friends and fellow rebels to an entire nation of teenagers. And it was the first novel I ever held onto long enough to finish. Once I had finished it, I reread it four times in the course of one year.

Holden Caulfield: the confused adolescent expelled from one private school after another; the boy angered and embittered by the death of his younger brother; and a very *real* friend with whom I shared a hatred for phony adults.

The book was engulfed in controversy for nearly two decades, during which time it was banned in many major cities and caused the firings of English teachers who dared to teach it. Back then, I would have wanted to be an English teacher about as much as I'd have wanted one of my eyes poked out. I still have both my eyes, although, strangely enough, I teach English to senior high school students every day of the work week. I've arranged with the powers-that-be to teach a one-semester minicourse entitled "Studies in Salinger," and every semester I cover the complete works of that author, including *Catcher, Nine Stories, Franny and Zooey*, and *Raise High the Roof Beam, Carpenters*. All of Salinger's books inspired near hysteria in bibliophiles, especially the younger ones, and resulted in lines at the stores on the day of each subsequent release. But there it ended. The 60-year-old author (he was born Jerome David Salinger on January 1, 1919) has been in hiding for nearly 25 years, and since 1965 his zealous fans have hungered—*starved*, actually—for another book, for one more spiritual journey anchored somewhere between urban youth and Zen.

He has promised. He has said, usually through his literary-agent spokesman, that more tales are coming. It was rumored for years that he was writing a trilogy featuring the Glass family, of which Franny and Zooey were but two out of seven precocious children. But nothing further was heard, and I recently became impatient. I started gathering essays and clippings about Salinger, which are rare indeed. I even spoke to the editor of a Chicago newspaper, who knew nothing of the ethereal writer's current life or work, and who suggested that finding the man would require nothing short of a minor miracle. So reclusive is Salinger that he has been known to run away from those who recognize him on the streets of his New England hometown.

Meanwhile, my class was constantly questioning me as

to further developments in the author's life. On the last day of the recent semester, one student asked, "Do you think he'll ever write again? Maybe he's just burned out."

"J. D. Salinger is *not* burned out!" I nearly screamed. It was the first and only time I have ever raised my voice to a student, and the only lesson I can find in the incident is that you don't suggest to a man surrounded by darkness that the only visible light on the horizon is in danger of extinguishing itself. I decided then and there to cease hovering around that one visible light and go directly to it. I had the summer off and the will to find old J.D.—all I needed was that minor miracle.

In the latest clip on Salinger, one that appeared in *The New York Times* on February 12, 1978, his agent was quoted as having said that the author was indeed writing actively every day, on his farm somewhere near Cornish, New Hampshire. I got out my atlas and located the town, which is so tiny, even on a blow-up of the state of New Hampshire, that it took me three hours to find it. My friends encouraged me to no end with helpful comments like "You're crazy. You'll never find him. He hasn't talked to outsiders in decades!" My mother was a bit kinder. She warned me to "take along some long underwear. It gets cold in those mountains, for God's sake."

With that advice in mind, I hit the road, intending to drive from Chicago and then camp out along the way to Cornish. The most notable occurrence during the trip involved my lack of experience with being alone at night in the woods.

I didn't mind that it rained all the way across the state of New York; but when the rain continued at an unprecedented rate while I was camping in the Adirondacks, my notes and map deteriorated before my very eyes.

The piece I read most nights in my tent was an anonymously published short story entitled "For Rupert—with No Promises." It appeared in the February 1977 issue of *Esquire*, and many Salinger aficionados have speculated that perhaps the famous recluse penned the story. The title is similar to one of his older works, "For Esme—with Love and Squalor," and throughout the newer tale in question, it is hinted that one writer is responsible for both pieces. The protagonist is fashioned after Zooey, and there are countless parallels and connections with other Salinger fiction. (I called former *Esquire* editor Lee Eisenberg, who verified that it was simply a takeoff. Eisenberg suspected that former fiction editor Gordon Lish had a hand in the writing. Lish has admitted as much since.)

One June 22, 1978, I drove into Cornish, New Hampshire. Realizing I was closer than I had ever been to Salinger, it did not seem out of the question to simply pull the car over next to any stranger and begin making inquiries. I did so upon spotting a long-haired, unsuspecting young man of about 25 years, who was casually walking by the side of the road. I stopped the car.

"J. D. Salinger? He's around here somewhere." I pressed for some more specific information.

"Well, I *did* go by his house once. It's way out in the sticks, up a bunch of dirt roads. Why don't you ask the guy at the little store just down the road? I think he knows him."

It wasn't hard to find the place; the little store is one of four institutions that make up the town of Cornish—not counting the farms. I walked in and the screen door banged behind me.

"Can I help you?" asked the store manager, a balding man who was looking over the top of his newspaper.

"Yeah. I need some peanut butter," I replied.

"Second aisle, last shelf. Need anything else?"

"Uh-huh. Could you tell me where I could find J. D. Salinger?"

The hospitality disappeared abruptly and the thought flashed through my mind that the local residents might feel loyally protective of their famous recluse.

"Well," he started, after a considerable pause in the conversation, "he used to live around here, not too far away. My wife, she has an autographed copy of *Franny and Zooey*. He brought it to her when she was in the hospital. He came right up and visited her because her folks used to be neighbors of his. You know what? I haven't heard nothin' about him in some time. But you go up to the flat; there's another store down the road and they might be able to help you."

I thanked him and wondered if I'd been thrown a red herring as I walked back to my overheated car. The flat—whatever that was—up the road—wherever that was.

I drove four more miles before coming to the next store. There were gas pumps out front, and above the establishment was a large, hand-painted sign: POWERS' STORE. I had been in Cornish all of ten minutes and I'd already come across two folks with at least marginal information. "Third time's a charm," I told myself.

Boy, was I right. Mr. Powers, a former stockbroker from

Boston, runs the store with his wife. I was fortunate enough to have come by while the part-time clerk, Ethel Nelson, was on duty. She not only knew the location of Salinger's old *and* new residences, but she also had been a baby-sitter for his two children many years ago. Ethel, who has a charming down-East accent and tons of personality, said the older home is a reddish farmhouse, which is now owned by J.D.'s former wife, Claire. She rents it out now, and is said to live somewhere in Pennsylvania. "She's a very nice woman," remarked Ethel with enthusiasm, "and *he* used to be full of life. He used to pick up us girls and take us to the Windsor High baseball games. He had a jeep and we'd all go to the games with him. But after he got rich and famous, well . . ."

I was admittedly shocked by her candor, but more especially by the implication of that remark. I chalked it up to carelessness as Ethel began writing directions to Salinger's house, a newer home just down the road from his former dwelling. Looking up occasionally, she added that he was now a bore and oftentimes cantankerous. My mouth fell open in a fit of incredulity, but I remained, thank God or something, silent.

"Watch out for the dogs," she said. They were supposed to be vicious, and J.D. was rumored to have a shotgun. At the mention of the gun I stopped in my tracks. According to Ethel, her mother had been collecting for the cancer drive not long before, and she had approached Salinger for a contribution. The gun came out, as did the dogs, but her mother reminded him that they had all known each other for years and said that she wasn't going to leave until he contributed. He is said to have eventually given five dollars.

While waiting for my directions, I noticed an old man sitting to my left at a small coffee counter, where customers routinely poured themselves cups of delicious country coffee. He wore wire-rimmed glasses, and the tufts of white hair that sparsely covered his head stood up at varying angles, causing him to look forever alarmed.

"J. D. Salinger," he said, nodding in my direction, "lives over on Dingleton Hill. I met him twenty-five years ago during the big fire. We helped put it out."

I thanked him for the information. From what I could gather, his name is Osworth. At least, that is what some of the customers called him as they entered and left.

Ethel then handed me a small piece of paper with street names listed in successive order. "Now, you be careful of those dogs," she said. "If you head toward the post office first, you may run into him picking up his mail. He drives a fancy new jeep and he's there every day at this time." She shook her head and added, "I feel like I'm sending you to your funeral."

I took the advice and headed straight for the post office. Desperately, I flashed reruns through my mind of the one still photo I'd ever seen of J. D. Salinger. It was in a dictionary of American authors, and I remembered the sad expression he wore, the large nose and protruding ears. I closely examined the faces of all the middle-aged men who were coming and going. After five minutes of close scrutiny, I became aware that two-thirds of the town of Cornish is made up of men in their 60s who drive fancy new jeeps. I literally thought that they were *all* Salinger. And I wished he had never grown old, wherever he was. I'd have liked to believe that he never changed from that young man who delivered autographed copies of his own book to hospital patients.

Feeling that my strategy was useless, I started the car once more and followed the hastily scribbled directions. They took me over a series of winding, unpaved roads lined with large, well-landscaped homes. One of the landmarks on the way to Salinger's hideout is a covered bridge that links Vermont and New Hampshire. Hence the frequent and inaccurate reports that the author lives somewhere in the Green Mountains of the former state.

Besides a ranch house with the name ORVILLE FITCH posted on the mailbox, I came across markers nailed to a stump. According to one of the markers, I had at last reached the top of Dingleton Hill. Ethel's directions proved rather confusing insofar as she perceived crossroads in terms of corners. "You'll come to three corners," the note read, but I couldn't tell what qualified as a full-fledge corner. I became so disoriented in the mazelike vicinity that I had to start over from scratch several times before I narrowed down the choices of likely residences to one. The prospective home was just down the road from the fabled farmhouse—his former abode. The driveway to the newer home is banked on a steep incline, and nowhere from street level is the structure visible; it is the perfect choice for a recluse of any variety. I jammed the gearshift into first and sped up the drive, leaving a cloud of dust behind me.

I found myself in the rocky front yard of a lovely but modest brown chalet with an upper balcony and a beautiful view of the Vermont mountains. The garage was directly in front of me, and I was about to get out of the car when three dogs—two golden retrievers and a German shepherd—ran down the balcony steps and surrounded me. They barked so loudly that I knew I had alerted any sensible, hearing person within a mile. And from my skimpy knowledge of dogs and their temperaments, I judged them to be fairly hostile. Pushing in the clutch, I rolled down the drive as quickly as I had climbed it, and then sped back down to the general store to verify my choice of houses.

I was greatly disappointed to find that Ethel had gone home for the evening. When the alternate clerk learned why I had come, she told me I should speak to the town clerk.

"Where can I find her?" I asked, exasperated by my day of playing amateur detective.

"She's right in back," replied the young woman, "working the meat counter."

The town clerk was indeed working the meat counter; I was at last getting a feel for how the small community took care of business. Her name is Bernice Johnson, and she is a quiet-toned, charming woman. She sized me up before answering my questions. I explained that I wanted to check my bearings as far as the location of Salinger's home, and she went right to work with a pencil, tracing the route on a simple map for me.

As it turned out, much to my surprise, Bernice is Orville Fitch's sister-in-law (remember the mailbox?). She has met Salinger quite a few times because he has to register his vehicles and dogs with her. On one occasion, she walked right up to his living-room window and rapped to get in; she'd had business to discuss and he'd proved to be most gentlemanly.

"Does he ever shoot at his visitors?" I asked.

"Hmmm . . . I don't think so. He's a very nice man—very

good about voting. But you have to understand, the man has been tormented so."

I did understand and I thanked her sincerely. Anybody who had taken so many steps to ensure his privacy, I reasoned, may well deserve it. I pondered that moral question as I drove out of Cornish the next day, bound for a visit to the anti-nuclear-power demonstration in Seabrook. I had left a letter, addressed to Salinger, with the local post office before I left town. In it I explained how hard I had been searching for him, how much I needed to speak to him, and how incredibly frightened of dogs I have *always* been. "A simple 'Leave!' will do it, Mr. Salinger," I wrote. "So please don't shoot at me." I said that I would return on Monday, the 26th of June, immediately after my stay in Seabrook.

Upon my return to Cornish, I stopped by the store one last time to have another chat with Ethel. She greeted me enthusiastically and sat me down at the coffee counter, saying she would return in a second. While I gathered my notes, I spotted an old, fat mongrel asleep next to the spaghetti shelf. Everything about Powers' Store was so quaint I fairly hoped my car would break down so that I'd have an excuse to spend more time there.

"That's our watchdog," Ethel said when she returned. "He doesn't look like much now, but he's a real terror at night."

"I'll bet," I said. "What's his name?"

"Dynamite."

I tape-recorded her responses so that my class could hear the information exactly as I had—inflections and New England accent intact. But when the recorder appeared, I found that she had taken on a new tone.

"I'm going to be very careful about what I say," Ethel warned me before we proceeded. I told her that would be fine. She put away some canned goods hurriedly, sat down at the counter and then eyed the recorder suspiciously.

"Well, he used to come down in his jeep, back when he wasn't married. He'd get sick of writing, so he'd come down whenever there was a big game at Windsor High School and pick up four or five of us girls to take us to the games.

"Mom never really cared for him. As far as she was concerned, he was a writer, and that made him lazy. She didn't like it a bit when we used to go to the games with him, and stuff. She thought that was *terrible*. He stayed right there with us, hollerin' and cheerin'—a very normal type human being, really. I mean, he was *fun*!

"He's been here thirty years. He's lived right in that area he lives in now. He used to live in that other house with the fence around it; that's where he and his wife lived and where his two kids were born. He says his books have nothing to do with his life—but being right there and seeing all those different things happening, like *Franny and Zooey*; he has a son and a daughter. It all just seems to fit right in there, even though he swears it has nothing to do with it. He said that to my husband. He said, 'It has nothing to do with my lifestyle; I just write out of my head.' Well, your head is your life, right? So it all just comes together. My husband worked for him after we were married. He worked on his studio."

Her point was nearly plausible; I had made the connection between the Windsor High games and the Pencey Prep games that Holden Caulfield mentions.

Ethel had me thoroughly hypnotized by then. Her pixie

face lit up during the reminiscences as if she were reliving
them. Dynamite even got up and sorely walked over to the
counter, though he only plopped himself down at our feet
and dozed off again.

"I don't know him today," she continued. "I haven't really talked with him in three years. I mean, he's just made
himself so aloof now. When you meet him on the road it's
just a nod, or once in a while—once in a *great* while, when
you least expect it—he'll all of a sudden be friendly and chat
for a few minutes.

"His kids are there a lot. You know, they're quite grown
up now; they're quite the young man and young lady. He
spoils them rotten, which you're supposed to do." She smiled.
"They must be—oh, God—she must be twenty-two and he
would be nineteen or twenty. Right up there, all grown up.
I baby-sat for them many times. *Smart* little kids. Very well
brought up; Claire did a beautiful job. And *she* did it! Jerry
was never there. He was always down in his studio, writing. And if he was in that studio writing, you *did not* call
him, even though there was an intercom between it and
the house. Unless there was an emergency, you did *not* pick
that up.

"I did that one day, not realizing it was this way. And
when Claire found out, she said, 'Don't ever do that again!'
But he didn't get mad. You see, the kids were insisting on
some such thing, and I didn't know just what to do; so I
buzzed the studio and he answered.

"Many times he gets all dressed up and puts on facial
things that make him not *him*."

"You mean he disguises himself?"

"Right, right! Many times. He once went to Hanover to a game like that—it's the only way he can do it without getting mobbed. Once the Hanover crowd starts seeing him, they're all over him. So he disguises himself and really gets away with it. I've seen him just once that way, and I knew him like *that* [*she snapped her fingers*] because I *know* him.

"He partakes of these things. If it's to do with the towns-people who know him and accept him, it's no big deal. He's just another John Doe as far as we're concerned. He doesn't impress us that much because he's here all the time. It's like Ascutney Mountain or St. Gauden's Memorial. They're here, so we accept them and that's it."

The latter-mentioned locations are two sight-seeing attractions that Cornish citizens are rather proud of. I inferred a little pride in Ethel's tone whenever she spoke of Salinger, also. He is to these people very much like Ascutney Mountain.

"God, when college kids come around trying to see him—*that* is grief. He just wants to be left alone. They had a big group come in from Boston. There were fifteen kids who came in, and they wanted to see him and interview him. That's when the gun first came out. His privacy was being invaded and these kids just insisted they had to talk to him! Now he has the dogs and the things to protect himself against this sort of thing.

"I don't know if he's still writing. The last book he wrote was turned into a movie. I didn't hear about this from him. I haven't heard of any of his writing since then."

I asked her if she knew the title of the movie.

"No—have not heard another word other than just that statement. It was turned into a movie, and he made a million on it."

Mrs. Powers, the store owner, was putting away the strawberries she had bought from a local farmer, and she broke into our conversation at this point.

"He's starting again, Ethel. He's writing a book now."

I immediately thought of the promised Glass family trilogy and wondered how she came by this information.

"Oh," Mrs. Powers began, "you just hear it. About two years ago, people were trying to get in to see him. They kept putting it in the paper. Then I thought, 'Gee, maybe he's writing another book.' Not much later I heard he *was* working on another one."

I asked Ethel if she knew the reason, or if she could guess at the reason Salinger had protected his privacy so carefully.

"I think he likes people, but he is much more famous by not being around all the time. Like you—look how hard you're trying to get to see him. And it isn't that he doesn't like you. If he comes out and talks to everybody, he's going to be just another writer who's very friendly."

Just another writer, I said to myself. No, I don't think he'll ever be just another writer. My own experience has taught me that something very special indeed flows through his prose. I've seen it work on my students in several different instances; the man is capable of changing lives through a story.

With these thoughts in mind, I finished my coffee and thanked both women again. They wished me luck and told me to let them know how it turned out.

As I drove up Dingleton Hill for the final time, I felt

partially acquainted with J.D. I found his home without problems this time; the tangled mess of inlets and side drives began to look familiar. I parked the car near the mouth of the drive and sat on the ground near his front yard for two hours. I am the only person I know of who keeps a complete library of Salinger works at all times in his glove compartment, and while I waiting to climb the driveway, I leafed leisurely through *Franny and Zooey*. I closed the book after some moments and stared at the cover. It is one thing to know an author simply by what he has written, and quite another to *know* him as a person. Once that line is crossed, it can never be reversed, and Salinger was about to become an entity different from what he had ever seemed to me before. He was about to be transformed from a familiar name on a dust jacket to a real human being, something altogether more frail and fallible. The prospect frightened me, but I had come too far to turn back.

It had begun to drizzle slightly as I got back into the car, nervously threw the gearshift into first, and quickly ascended the drive. I parked in front of the garage and turned off the engine. The dogs came running down the balcony steps and I rolled up the windows as fast as I could. They barked so intensely that I didn't notice that the garage door had started to rise. I did a double take when, from beneath the small portion already opened, two knees became visible. The door continued to rise slowly; I made out the waistline of a man in gray slacks, then a blue, short-sleeved shirt and, finally, a gaunt, line-ridden face. He stared directly at me and walked slowly toward my car in the cool rain. J. D. Salinger had materialized, it seemed, out of nowhere. His hair was full but gray, and he stood for a moment unspectacularly next to his jeep. He again walked toward me. His gait was slow but strong, and as he approached, I half hoped he was the gardener. I rolled down the window and looked up into the most touching face I have ever encountered. It was a face deeply carved; his eyes seemed to be sunken, yet they bore down upon me with a blue translucence. Compared to this, Holden, Seymour, and the entire cast of his characters were dwarfed. If we had never talked to each other, never exchanged one word, I at least knew the sound of one hand clapping.

"You mean you dared to come up here and face these ferocious beasts?" he asked, as he began laughing and stroking the head of his German shepherd. The dog wagged its tail and sat down next to him. I was relieved temporarily.

"Are you the man who wrote the letter?"

I said yes, I had written the letter.

"It was a rather humorous note. What is it you want to know? What are your questions?"

It began to rain harder; yet he stood near my car window with raindrops on his face. His voice was demanding, and I was fairly uncertain as to what I had wanted to know in the first place. I explained that my main concern was whether or not he was still actively writing.

"Yes, of course!" He seemed surprised. "What do you think I do? I'm a writer. But my communication with the public is through my fiction. Contact with the public hinders my work. This has been a problem with some of my colleagues, and it has hurt them."

"I understand that—" I started, but he interrupted me, his tall, thin frame tightening slightly.

"No, you don't. No, you don't understand that. *If you did, you wouldn't be here.*"

"You're right, you're right. I'm sorry. I don't mean to intrude," I admitted. I was completely off-balance. He had taken me by surprise when he had asked, nearly painfully, what I wanted. It was as if he'd had to ask the same question of hundreds of searchers, who could never quite determine, once they were up there, exactly what they had wanted.

"Look," I insisted, "your work has meant a lot to me and to my students. We read the clippings—the ones that say you're here, that you're writing. People come to *me* to find out about *you* because they love what you write."

He looked at the ground for a second, then said, "That's very kind."

"But it's been a long time since you've published anything," I reminded him.

"Yes," he agreed, as he looked at the ground once more, "it has been some time. But I cannot be rushed. Publication is an agonizing thing to go through. It takes at least a year and a half *after* publication to get back in stride. It's a tremendous obstacle."

The rain again became heavy, and somehow I felt his mood had lightened.

"Will there be any published stories in the near future?"

"I can't predict publication dates," he said firmly.

"Well, should I go back and tell them there is something to hope for? That there is at least hope that there will eventually be more stories?"

He became enthusiastic here and looked up suddenly, saying, "Oh, yes, yes. There will be more. There is hope for more." He seemed to examine the backseat of my car every so often. I had camping gear sprawled all over, and I suspect he was looking for recording equipment or cameras. I had deliberately locked them in the trunk to keep from scaring him away.

"So, you just came back from there?" he asked. I gathered he meant Seabrook, because I had mentioned in the letter that I intended to visit the coastal city.

"Yes, it was very nice. Thousands of people and not a hint of violence. They were all very supportive of each other; it was kind of nice to see."

He smiled and nodded, a grin beginning to form across his mouth. The earlier sarcastic and somewhat gruff tone had vanished and he now appeared very shy.

"Was our dear Governor Meldrim Thomson there?" he wanted to know. I guess he hadn't read the paper. I told him no, the man had not shown up, but that there had been several jokes made at the New Hampshire executive's expense. Again he shook his head and smiled.

"I don't want to keep you in the rain," I said. His clothes were thoroughly soaked and little drops were gathering on his face.

"Well, I don't know what else I can tell you. Everything I have to say is in my fiction."

I told him he had been very helpful, and asked him to forgive the inconvenience. He shook my hand and I gave his a long, hardy clasp. I watched as he walked back to the garage, though my mind was far away. I was recalling two passages that I think clarify his desire to remain aloof, away from center stage.

The first passage I had in mind is from "A Perfect Day for Bananafish," when Seymour asks a woman passenger on an elevator not to stare at his feet. The next one is from *Zooey*, and it is that character's demand that his mother, Bessie Glass, stop admiring his back. The physical presence in both instances is unimportant to Salinger; it is the spiritual *essence* that he wishes his readership would notice and value.

He called his dogs to him and waved while the rain splashed on the gravel. I waved back and started the car, with yet another scene from his work spinning loosely in my memory. It was from *Catcher in the Rye*, when Phoebe is going around and around on a carousel in the falling rain, while Holden is just sitting there on the bench getting soaked.

"I didn't care, though . . ." Holden says. "I felt so damn happy, if you want to know the truth. I don't know why . . . God, I wish you could have been there."

AFTERWORD BY GREG HERRIGES

I was only twenty-eight, though I had been a high school English teacher for six years in the Chicago public school system. It was a career that chose me rather than the other way around because I had fallen in love with literature. One novel held a special place in not just my heart but in my reader's soul as well: *The Catcher in the Rye*.

Like Holden, I had some rather gaping voids in my life. My father had recently passed away, and my first marriage had failed grandly. But there was some good news along the way: I had just published my first magazine article in *The Chicago Tribune Sunday Magazine*, "Inherit the Streets," an inside look at the city's street gangs. And because of that I appeared as a featured guest on an hour-long segment of Charlie Rose's *A.M. Chicago*, a lucky break for a fellow with hopes of being a writer.

Talk about big dreams—I wanted to follow in Salinger's footsteps. I'd read all of his works, including the twenty-two uncollected stories. I was visiting a friend of mine at lunchtime in a bookstore in Kenilworth, Illinois, when a fellow walked in and asked us if we wanted to buy any books by J. D. Salinger. We told him we owned all of Salinger's books, and he said, "No, you don't." He was peddling the uncollected stories in two unauthorized volumes from the trunk of his car. Of course we both bought them, and they became my writer's textbook. I didn't just read them, I *studied* them, *memorized* them. I was a literary evangelist; I could quote passages of the holy texts at will.

Every night I would click away at my typewriter turning out yet another Salinger counterfeit, learning my craft by blatantly imitating my unknowing mentor. I was a devoted protégé, albeit a remarkably naïve one. But that is how we learn, yes?

After Dorothy Olding, Salinger's literary agent, let it slip to an Associated Press reporter that Salinger was writing every day at his house in Cornish, New Hampshire, I was off like a rocket. But the real story was more complicated and dramatic than the version I could tell forty years ago. My girlfriend was with me the whole time. Her former boyfriend followed us from Chicago, or perhaps she told him where we were going. Early one morning, while we were camping, he surprised us. I hate surprises, especially surprises like that. We ended up driving back to Chicago through Canada to keep him off our trail. That trip was the longest break-up of my life; it went on for days and miles and I thought it would never end. At my girlfriend's request, I erased her from the narrative until I wrote *JD: A Memoir of a Time and a Journey* (Wordcraft of Oregon, 2006).

When I recount my Salinger story for students, they always have the same question: "Why did he come out and talk to *you* when so many others had been unsuccessful?"

The answer: *the letter.* It was the letter that I wrote to him and mailed from the Windsor, Vermont, post office. I composed that letter in a campground about three miles down the road from Salinger's home, and I knew what it would have to do—it would have to open the door for me. It would have to allay his fears, appeal jointly to his senses of curiosity and humor, and in the process it would have to entertain. I had an instinctual awareness of the level of humor and irony that Salinger would appreciate, that he practiced himself. When you have been immersed in the musings of another person's psyche for an extended period of time—that is, after all, what is going on when you read someone else's written work at length—you have experienced an intensely intimate connection. By the time I had a working copy of that letter, I was certain that Salinger would see me. I just knew it.

I have a regret or two about not having probed a bit deeper during our conversation. I wish I had inquired about some of the early stories, such as "The Stranger" or "Personal Notes of an Infantryman"—the war stories. My Uncle Lenny had been killed five years before I was born in a battle that Salinger had survived in the Hürtgen Forest. Did the uncle I never knew and the author I admired most ever meet? Most likely not; we're talking about thousands and thousands of men just trying to stay alive under the worst imaginable circumstances. I wish I would have known how to broach the subject without upsetting him, but I simply did not have the skill to do it. Nothing but minefields in that direction. Perhaps if I had been more mature, if I had had the perspective I possess today—but if that had been the case, I wouldn't have undertaken such a journey in the first place.

No matter. When I look back across the blurry terrain of so many years it surprises me how quickly it was over, that meeting that has proven so important to my life and my chosen line of work—teaching and writing. I am sixty-six now, a full professor of English at William Rainey Harper College in Palatine, Illinois. If I hadn't fallen for *The Catcher in the Rye* as a teenager, if I hadn't been successful in meeting Salinger, I don't know what I would have done, or exactly what I would have become.

It was a flash, but for me a very satisfying one that hasn't lost any of its immediate effulgence, even after all that time. Salinger came out and he talked to me, was kind to me—kind but stern. I think he wanted me to know just how lucky I was that he had deigned to grant me an audience. I can't fault him for that. It was quite a gift. I was allowed for a few minutes to witness my literary hero in action, to see the way he comported himself, to hear his elegant New England spoken inflections, and to measure and be intimidated by his somewhat haughty manner. And we shook hands; I actually touched him. In the most meaningful of figurative ways, he touched me as well.

"IF YOU'RE LONELY, AS MOST WRITERS ARE, WRITE YOUR WAY OUT OF IT."

INTERVIEW BY MICHAEL CLARKSON
NIAGARA FALLS REVIEW
NOVEMBER 12, 1979

I sat in my car in Cornish, N.H., and waited. I was parked on a quiet, unpaved country lane known only to the local volunteer rescue squad. Ferns pressed against the car in the narrow green tunnel, and white birches creaked overhead. There was no sign or mailbox at the foot of the long, spiral driveway leading uphill from my waiting place; in fact, feeling a bit like I was trapped in "The Three Bears," I wasn't even sure there was a house at the secret summit, or if the man I was tracking was barricaded, bearded, in the concrete bunker the stories described.

I wondered if I was further ahead than the teenager who hitchhiked from Sacramento, the woman from Europe proposing marriage, the world's crack reporters and investigators, or the thousands who had their letters defaulted, unopened, in a post office wastebasket, all without getting the time of day from J. D. Salinger since he went into seclusion in 1953.

Salinger stopped publishing at the peak of his fiction career in 1965 at the age of 46, creating the biggest riddle in the history of American letters. He has never answered his fans or critics and has been known to flee if approached by a stranger.

After reading Salinger's novel, *The Catcher in the Rye*, I had a warm, intimate feeling for the author, but here, sweating apprehensively in a trench coat after a 450-mile drive, I felt like an intruder.

Inspired by a remark in *Catcher* from Salinger's alter ego, Holden Caulfield ("I'd pretend I was one of those deaf-mutes. That way I wouldn't have to have any goddamn stupid useless conversations with anybody. If anybody wanted to tell me something, they'd have to write it on a piece of paper and shove it over to me"), I had given a note for the recluse to a clerk in the variety store where he was rumored to occasionally surface to buy newspapers. My note, product of two months' labor, read: "A man is in Cornish. Amateur, perhaps, but sentimentally connected. The saddest—a tragic figure without a background. Needing a future as much as your past. Let me."

Without warning, two European compacts varoomed from an opening in the bush. Sharply they braked near my car. A long-haired teenager sprang from the lead vehicle and, referring to the other driver as "Dad," faced me with a karate stance and three howling dogs at his flanks.

A tall, thin, graying man emerged confidently from a gray BMW with a soccer sticker on its bumper. With a wave, he signaled the boy and the dogs away. A regimented, military walk brought the man, dressed neatly in a brown tweed jacket with leather patches on the elbows, black turtleneck, and sneakers, to my window.

"Are you J. D. Salinger?" I managed to ask.

"Yes. What can I do for you?" he said earnestly through enamel-white dentures. It couldn't be Salinger. For one thing, a photograph taken 27 years before resembled somebody else; for another, he looked older than 59.

"I don't know. I was hoping you could tell me."

"Oh, c'mon, don't start that."

"Really. All I know is I left my family and job and came a long way to see you."

"You didn't quit, did you?"

I shook my head.

"Are you under psychiatric care?"

"No. I don't think that's the problem. I suppose I have a need to be published," I said, as best I could, considering my suspected mental derangement. "It's hard finding people I feel comfortable with, who I can share with." (Holden in *Catcher*: "What really knocks me out is a book that, when you're all done reading it, you wish the author that wrote it was a terrific friend of yours and you could call him up on the phone whenever you felt like it.")

"You'll eventually find somebody," he said, trying to make my life seem as important as his. A dignity exuded from him, from his deep, nasal, studious voice—bordering British—to his drooping ears and fleshy nose. He seemed weather-beaten, homely but in an attractive way; a distinguished clown whose soul didn't have to be painted on his face, but was projected through the serious expression and dark, faraway eyes.

"Anyway, how do you know you'd be comfortable with me?" His forehead and eyebrows, outstanding beneath a thick mixture of gray and white hair, slicked straight back, were tight with what seemed like worry, or at least a headache.

"Your writing."

He grew 6 inches taller. "I'm a fiction writer!" As if a nerve had been bared, he pushed away from the window to display outstretched hands. "There's absolutely no autobiography in my stories. I've had those notes passed around before," he said with a pained wince. "They're self-destructive, you must get out of that frame of mind." Confused, I didn't answer.

"Do you have another source of income besides writing?" he asked in an outgoing style. I kept waiting for him to introduce me to the man I'd come to see.

"I'm a reporter, police beat," I said. He was back in his car before I could blow smoke down my nose. "But I'm here for myself, not my job." My voice broke.

"I certainly hope so because I don't have it coming!" he announced, eyes contemptuous. For the first time in my life I felt really hated . . . and feared. "I've made my stand clear. I'm a private person, why can't my life be my own? I never asked for this and have done absolutely nothing to deserve it. I've had 25 years of this—I'm sick of it!" His delivery, timing, and flair superbly fit the message. It was almost like acting.

Dramatically he left in a hail of pebbles and surprised me again—by elevating his gangling arm up through the open roof for a friendly wave.

In a few minutes, as I sat dumbfounded, the man I couldn't be certain wasn't A. J. Foyt returned and issued warnings about having me removed. I told him I'd written another note. "Bring it here," he snapped. I left my car and walked to his window for a change. The long arm reached for the note and another produced a pair of glasses from a case.

The note, digested with his heavy lower lip naturally ajar, seemed to embarrass him: "Jerry: I'm sorry. It was probably a mistake coming to Cornish. You're not as deep, as sentimental, as I had hoped. If someone had driven 12 hours after leaving his family and job, I'd sure have given him more than five minutes. If I was after a story, do you think I would have told you I was a reporter? You say you're a fiction writer, but when you touch other people's souls, there's more to it than that. The person who wrote those books I love (Signature.) P.S. I'll be staying at the Windsor Motel until morning."

He shut his motor off, including the one in his car, and spoke softly, extra slowly. He seemed ready to burst into tears as he sat in his car and looked away from me. "Yes, well, you have the right to be cynical . . . but I've gone through this so many times, there's no gracious way to tell you to leave. I'm becoming embittered." When he pulled an ugly face, somehow it didn't look right.

The things I was asking him, telling him, he'd heard over and over again, he said, more to the trees and posterity than to me, head shaking wearily, his dialogue conservative and tightly edited, with no room for small talk. "The words are a little different each time. People with problems, people needing to communicate, people wanting help for their careers. They've come from all over this country, Canada, and Europe. They've collared me in elevators, on the street, here. Why, I've even had to turn and run from them. I get stacks of mail and questions every day."

I thought of another passage in *Catcher*:

Anyway, I keep picturing all these little kids playing some game in this big field of rye and all. Thousands

of little kids, and nobody's around—nobody big, I
mean—except me. And I'm standing on the edge of
some crazy cliff. What I have to do, I have to catch
everybody if they start to go over the cliff—I mean
if they're running and they don't look where they're
going I have to come out from somewhere and *catch*
them. That's all I do all day. I'd just be the catcher in
the rye and all. I know it's crazy, but that's the only
thing I'd really like to be.

His game face dissolved, he slapped his hands on the
steering wheel and squeezed it repeatedly. "There are no gen-
eralizations. You grew up under different circumstances than
I did; you had different parents. I'm not a teacher or a seer,
anyway. I pose questions a little differently, perhaps. But I
don't pretend to know the answers." He constantly referred to
his career in the present tense.

"Nothing one man can say can help another. Each must
make his own way. For all you know I'm just another father
who has a son." His eyes were a day's work to look into. It
would have helped him, I thought, if he could have cried
publicly. I considered offering him a cigarette, but there was
no sign of the chain-smoking reported in his early years.
"When I started in this business I had no idea this was going
to happen. In ways, I regret ever having been published; it's
the insanest profession. If you're lonely, as most writers are,
write your way out of it."

He said he couldn't give me "a magic quarter to put under my pillow to make me a successful writer by morning,"
but he kept talking about writing. "You can't teach somebody

how to write, it's the blind leading the blind," he stated. For a time after enrolling in a short-story course in 1939, his prose was said to suffer from a workmanlike falsity. "The only good thing about lectures is they offer you a chance to mingle with others who've had rejection slips and share something in common." He wasn't being funny. Odd, how I considered us both to have a sense of humor, yet in all the time we talked, neither of us laughed.

He claimed writing was still an open field to those "with enough drive and ego" and that publishers still took time to read salable material. I wondered if he knew what it was like to have manuscripts returned, to be unloved creatively. To have no feedback. "Writing for yourself can be rewarding," he said. "But if you want to be published, I'll tell you this— you'll never be an author from the words I saw on that note at the store. Nobody over 30 can make head nor tail of that cryptic language. You have to separate fact from fiction."

"Would a writing career be worth it in the long run?" I asked.

"Sure, if that's what you want."

"Sometimes I lose incentive."

"Write your way out of it. Put everything down. Otherwise I have no answers for you."

I left when I decided I was standing below J. D. Salinger's driveway and not at the bottom of some crazy cliff.

Jerome David Salinger, the most influential literary force of the 1950s and early '60s, was followed by irony from his birth in New York City in 1919 on the most public day of the year, January 1. His Irish-Jewish parents were the owners of a prosperous ham-importing business, and his only sibling, Doris, was a dress buyer. As an introverted, polite child of average IQ, he liked to act and write and go for long walks by himself, but didn't apply himself at school, flunking out of several.

After a brief fling at writing Army publicity releases, Staff Sgt. Salinger won five battle stars with the U.S. Fourth Division intelligence in World War II. All aspects of the fighting demoralized him (including a visit from war correspondent Ernest Hemingway, who tried to impress people by decapitating a chicken with a German Luger), but it was in Europe that his first real writings were born—in the foxholes between shellings. Some of the profits from magazine sales to *Collier's*, *Esquire*, and *The Saturday Evening Post* were sent home to be used to encourage new writers.

By 1948 Salinger had won a contract with the prestigious *New Yorker* magazine, with stories about heartache—the frustrating search for peace and undiscriminating non-sexual love in a world where childhood innocence was sadly perverted by adulthood and sincerity corroded by fame. But the critics agreed: somehow his stories held hope for mankind.

The author talked of making it big in movies until Hollywood in 1950 altered his short story "Uncle Wiggly in Connecticut" into "My Foolish Heart." He has since rejected all offers from filmmakers, television, and stage groups—even book clubs—and blocks all attempts by editors to publish unpolished stories of his early career.

With his only novel, the tragicomic *Catcher* (1951), which speaks—shouts—out against social and academic conformity,

Salinger became an instant hero to students all over the world. The book, about Holden Caulfield, a sensitive 16-year-old who flees school in pursuit of meaningful contacts only to find a world riddled with phonies, affected the vernacular of a generation and has been banned by some school boards for its obscenity and apparent support of rebellion.

Overwhelming reaction to *Catcher* had not eased by 1953, when Salinger, now 34 and deeply involved in Zen Buddhism, bought an un-winterized saltbox house in Cornish, N.H., where he was happy to pump his own water and could quench his thirst for 1930s movies at the nearby Dartmouth College Film Society. Outgoing, he invited acquaintances for yoga sittings and befriended high school students, jeeping them to basketball games and entertaining them at record parties over Cokes and his favorite tune, "It Was Just One of Those Things." "All of my best friends are children," he once said.

One afternoon in 1953 he gave an unprecedented interview to a 16-year-old girl for the high school page of the local paper. The day after it was given prominence on the editorial page and flashed across the country, Salinger severed relations with the students and built a high fence around his house, claiming he needed isolation to keep his creativity intact. Few people have seen him since.

Also in 1953, *Nine Stories*, all he wished preserved from his first 29 short stories, was printed in book form. Two years later he married English-born Claire Douglas, a popular, attractive Radcliffe graduate. They had two children, Margaret, born in 1955, and Matthew, in 1960.

For the next 12 years Salinger lived for two families,

his own and the fictional Glasses, and, sustained by packed lunches, often spent more time with the latter, writing up to 18 hours a day—in a special concrete bunker 100 yards from the house—about the complex world of the introspective Glass family, nice people seeking religious peace in a cruel society, whose jugglings with Zen taught them every person was as important as the next, even the grotesque "Fat Lady."

Salinger got so lost in his work at times that it nearly involved him in automobile accidents. Edith Taylor, wife of an English teacher who closely followed Salinger's career, recalls the author "swaying all over the road in his jeep, having deep conversations and quarrels with himself."

The Glasses first appeared in sophisticated stories in *The New Yorker*, then were collected in the books *Franny and Zooey* (1961) and *Raise High the Roofbeam, Carpenters*, and *Seymour: An Introduction* (1963). The books, translated around the world, sold out immediately, and his enormous success, despite his not offering one word of publicity on his own behalf, became a contradiction of, a joke on, American life. Here was a man who, at the height of his fame, the target of every major reporter and Ph.D. candidate, kept a simple, unlocked mailbox with a stenciled name tag in front of his house.

No other writer since the Hemingway–Fitzgerald era had aroused so much public and critical interest, pro and con. Everybody had an opinion on J. D. Salinger. But he has never responded to his critics.

Salinger's production remained meager because of the fanatical editing and polishing he employed to make his stories tight as violin strings; he was accused of agonizing days over the choice of a solitary word. With "Hapworth 16, 1924," a story published in *The New Yorker* in 1965 about modern-day saint Seymour Glass, the career ended, although he once told a friend he intended to write a lengthy trilogy on the Glasses, a sort of "American *Remembrance of Things Past.*"

The New Yorker thought enough of his drawing power to keep him on a huge annual retainer fee (rumored to be $30,000), while a publicity stunt in 1977 by *Esquire*, which printed a story laced with hints that it was composed by The Great Recluse, reportedly received the heaviest responses of any piece in the magazine's history. Salinger still keeps an agent, Dorothy Olding of Harold Ober Associates in New York, but she, like all his editors, is mum about his career.

Warren French, a Midwest professor who moved to Cornish after writing a book-length study of Salinger, says he's surprised Salinger has never tried to form his own movie company, ". . . but I guess that would involve working with other people."

Claire was awarded the children and the house when she was granted a divorce from Salinger in 1967, but the author built a new home across the road and remained close to his family, visiting them daily.

In the meantime, enough has trickled out about his personal life to suggest he inserted parts of his history and lifestyle into his fiction. Most of his characters, seemingly more real and believable than he in their parallel world, are puritanical figures, standing for ideals in cement shoes, who would quit school, skip their weddings, and shoot themselves in the right temple rather than compromise. Yet unlike the author, interestingly, most of them are extroverted windbags.

PART TWO

It wasn't until a full year after I first met Salinger that I nerved myself to follow him up the steep driveway.

What I found at the top was beautiful—a rambling, dark-wooden lodge, nearly a Swiss chalet, not unlike one Caulfield had pined for ("I'd build me a little cabin somewhere in the woods with the dough I made . . . I'd build it right near the woods, but not right *in* them, because I'd want it to be sunny as hell all the time"). It was nestled up the side of a cliff at the edge of the woods in bright sunlight with enough windows for a greenhouse. There was no visible entrance from the long grass, but a concrete tunnel led conspicuously from a locked, two-car garage up the cliff, past a bird feeder and under a wide sun deck.

His dogs sniffed, but stopped barking. I scaled the least hazardous side of the rock and made it to the back of the Tyrolean structure, where I found wooden steps leading up to a set of heavy sliding glass doors. And I climbed, determination denying my nervousness.

Hands visored to my eyes, I squinted through the glass . . . into a living room so old-fashioned and tattered I expected to see ghosts. A hanging light set the depressing atmosphere, centering several old, worn couches and easy chairs, a bookcase, and a thin, patterned red rug that were dwarfed in the spacious room. A movie screen on the far wall was pulled halfway down to the floorboards, which were obviously older than the house. Sunshine, as it was in the Glass apartment, was unkind to the room. Disarray was the theme, with large metal spools of movie film, books, and *National Geographic*s scattered about. A large fireplace was clotted with crumpled writing paper and garbage.

But the dominant force was framed photographs, black and white, brown and yellow, spilling over the fireplace mantel and onto end tables. They were mostly group shots of his children and ex-wife, who had recently sold their old house and moved to the West Coast, and I couldn't keep the words of critic Arthur Mizener out of my head: "The fact that the Glass family is large and closely knit is also important to the feelings Salinger cares most about. The essential reality for him subsists in personal relations, when people, however agonizingly, love one another."

You could almost smell the mustiness through the glass. The room was surprising for a man wealthy from royalties: *Catcher* alone reportedly still sells 250,000 copies a year.

The owner was at ease on a chair facing another set of glass doors—the room was circled with them—watching a portable TV and writing on a pad. I knew he'd be home. He only leaves for necessities or if there happens to be a fire, I had learned in the interim. Each weekday he drives to the nearest settlement—Windsor, VT. (population 4,000), his lifeline to the world for a quarter of a century—and makes three hurried stops: the post office, Grand Union supermarket, and the Windsor Newsstand (he stopped buying his *New York Times* at Brooks Beauty and Health Aids after I passed my note through the clerk there). He was said to treat the newsstand employees "politely and gently" and the women "gallantly." He even offered his name as reference to a teen-age clerk seeking employment elsewhere.

On the street, unrecognized by most, he is a lonely, al-most pitiful figure, with fright, not spring, in his walk (a very unmilitary walk), rushing as if he is on Mars and his air isn't going to last him home. If you see him before he sees you, and he's been your boyhood idol, you want to go home and cry a little.

"People want to get close to him," an official of the Windsor Chamber of Commerce said, "but he wears his privacy like a balloon. You're afraid if you get beyond superficial conversation, it'll burst." A retired Cornish neighbor believes, "Everybody wants to be like Salinger and he wants to be like everybody else."

"He used to live in here," said a waitress at Nap's Lunch. "The kids listened like disciples to every word he said. They still read his stuff, but now he might as well be a writer who lives 2,000 miles away."

Not everyone approves of Salinger's lifestyle, but most so fear his opinion of them that they demand their comments remain anonymous. "He's speaking to me again," sighed a retired English teacher, blamed by Salinger for putting a *Time* magazine reporter on his trail years ago.

The indefatigable reporters who still make the long trek up here each year get no help from the *Windsor Chronicle*, the weekly tabloid that has, according to publisher Nancy Walker, an established policy "to respect the man's privacy" and has never done a story about him. Salinger's voice has been heard publicly only once in the last 14 years: *The New York Times* reported a 1974 telephone call from him protesting the efforts of a San Francisco group to publish an unauthorized collection of his stories. It has been said that the only letters he answers are from a prisoner at Sing Sing.

Salinger spotted me at the glass and stepped around a

sleeping German shepherd before impatiently kicking out a
2-by-4 that held the clear doors shut. He had aged in the year
since I'd seen him: the lines in his forehead and cheeks were
deeper. He wore faded blue jeans, tennis shoes, and a white
shirt, the sleeves rolled up to the bony elbows. He still looked
like he had a headache.

I thanked him for having helped me into a more realistic
frame of mind.

"You look much better now," he said from that slow face.
He smiled after I smiled, but he stood round-shouldered
in the door as if protecting his depressing room. "Are you
still reporting?" I nodded. "You tried to bully me last time,"
he said. "You tried to use me for the betterment of your
career. The only advice I can give is to read others, get what
you can out of a book, and make your own interpretation
of what the author is saying. Don't get hung up on the critics and that madness. Blend in your experiences, without
writing facts, and use your creativity. Plan your stories and
don't make rash decisions. Then, when it's finished, you're
in your own stew . . ." he lectured, head and hands ani-
mated. He looked like he was beginning to enjoy himself,
but suddenly he stopped in the middle of a sentence and
waited for me to talk. J. D. Salinger, Windbag? It had a certain ring to it.

As I looked out onto the sunlit reality of green hills and
vales, I was enveloped in a feeling of freedom and openness.
How could there be anything to conceal out here? "I'm sorry
if I bothered you before," I said.

"If you'd have written beforehand, I would have saved
you the bother of a long trip."

"I did. Five times. Didn't you get the tape of music relating to your career?"

"Tape?" he emptied his face of expression. "I might have. It was probably with the other stuff."

"Your writing seems to form attachments in its readers," I said.

"But I can't be held responsible," he shot out. "There are no legal obligations. I have nothing to answer for." His works were written for enjoyment and entertainment, he said with an overkill of emphasis, not for study or psychoanalysis.

"You haven't really given an explanation to your fans why you ran from them, then stopped publishing."

He raised his eyebrows. "Being a public writer interferes with my right to a private life. I write for myself."

"Don't you want to share your feelings?"

"No, that's wrong." He pointed his finger like a gun. "That's where writers get in trouble." He didn't have to be standing inside for the last paragraph of *Catcher* to haunt him: "I'm sorry I told so many people about it . . . It's funny. Don't ever tell anybody anything. If you do, you start missing everybody."

Before leaving, I invited him to come with me for a drink one night. "Thanks, but no." He smiles, almost mischievously, with the actor's flair. "I'm busy these days."

The door closed and Jerome David Salinger, the closet sentimentalist, retreated again. Not to a small town in New England or even into his lonely cabin, but to the safety of his head.

AFTERWORD BY MICHAEL CLARKSON

J. D. Salinger was the second man I ever loved. The first was my father, Fred, who couldn't or wouldn't love me enough. But why did I follow Salinger into the deep woods? Why did I leave my family, my job, and my sanity to drive four hundred and fifty miles to kiss his ring when he wanted only to be a deaf-mute? Salinger demanded the answers when I met him below his driveway. "Are you under psychiatric care?" he asked.

Me nuts, Jerry? Hey, I'll admit I may have been lonely for you and your intimate ideas, but aren't you the guy who quit publishing at the height of his career because he couldn't stand his critics and fans? Wasn't it you who holed up in a house without heat or water? Wasn't it you who was afraid of leaving home, of others' opinions, of aging?

For the next twenty-five minutes in that visit of 1978, I engaged the world's most celebrated literary neurotic in a game of fan-author ping-pong, then we continued the game one year later. Okay, he got lucky with the guess about my shrink. Over the next twenty-five years, through three therapists and anti-depressants and courses in fear and psychology, I finally had to admit that I was at least a depressive and perhaps (this is going to hurt me more than you) narcissistic.

Before I met Salinger, I spent ten years doing freelance sports writing in Fort Erie, Ontario, for two small daily newspapers, a weekly newspaper, and the *Buffalo Evening News*. When I got married in 1973, Jennifer and I could not afford to buy a home. At one point, she got a job at a department store while I freelanced and stayed home during the day with our infant son Paul. I tried to make it as a fiction writer at night with stories about relationships and complex, sometimes misunderstood characters, some of them suicidal.

We knew we could not get ahead with this set-up so we moved twenty miles up the Niagara River to Niagara Falls, but I had to give up my freelance markets and went on welfare for several months. We had our second son, Kevin, and I went home from the hospital depressed because we really couldn't afford to give him a good life. Eventually, I got two short-term jobs, one mowing grass and cleaning washrooms for the Niagara Parks Commission, where my father worked as a carpenter, and the other on a government grant for Mental Health Niagara Falls. Yeah, let's hire the depressed guy and see how that works out.

I don't know what my job description was. I was on the side of the desk where the sane people were supposed to be, and I helped out with about a dozen people who came in with emotional and mental problems. We played darts in the basement and horseshoes outside, trying to keep their anger managed while they had projectiles in their hands. One chap, Dennis, seemed to take a liking to me. He had had some problem in the past with a meat cleaver and said to watch out for his anger if he put gloves on. Another guy, Peter, had some serious problems, but he was harmless and would go around all day chanting things like: "If you see Marnie"—a social worker at the hospital—"I don't mind her golden hair." He repeated things and sometimes resembled Dustin

Hoffman's autistic character in the movie *Rain Man*, but he seemed to love coming and playing darts ("It's an easy game, an easy game"). The patients somehow reminded me of a side of Holden Caulfield, who was in what was then called a mental home when he narrated *The Catcher in the Rye*. Maybe I could take Dennis and Peter with me to see J. D. Salinger. They certainly made me feel better.

I landed a full-time reporting job with the *Niagara Falls Review*, even though the publisher, Gordon Murray, said my earlier freelance stories had been "riddled with clichés." Yikes. At first, I enjoyed the job, especially with the Canadian Press ticker rattling all day in a corner, although I did not have the freedom of freelancing and I was too tired at night to do much fiction writing. I was on the police beat and Niagara Falls was beautiful but tacky, with lots to write about in suicides over the falls, hookers, and drugs flowing across the New York border.

Two of my other problems were they worked you like a bum and I was putting in way too much overtime—the fire trucks tooted their horns passing my house at 4 a.m. to alert me to arsonists. I felt I had no one to relate to philosophically (what's new?). I became close to another reporter at the *Review*, although we did not have a physical affair. Maybe I should have seen a psychologist. Instead, I went to see J. D. Salinger.

At the time, I didn't even know he was alive, until I read a wire service story out of Boston in the *Toronto Globe and Mail* about a mysterious, unsigned story which had just appeared in *Esquire* magazine with clues that it might have been written by Salinger. Apparently the fifty-nine-year-old Salinger was living as a recluse in New Hampshire and had published nothing in thirteen years, although his agent said he was still writing. Apparently, he had an unlisted phone number; otherwise, there was no biographical information I could use, no clues to find him. But maybe there were clues in Holden's words in *Catcher*: "If anybody wanted to tell me something, they'd have to write it on a piece of paper and shove it over to me."

I wrote a letter and put together a tape of songs:

Summer 1977

Dear J. D.: I hope you don't mind my writing and disturbing you, but I feel I have known you a long time . . . enclosed please find a tape of music I think relates to your career.

Cheers,
Michael Clarkson

Included were snippets of Cole Porter's "Just One of Those Things," The Platters' "Smoke Gets in Your Eyes" (a song his characters liked), Robert Burns's "Comin' Thro' the Rye," Tommy Dorsey's "Song of India" (relating to his love of eastern religions), Vera Lynn's "If You Love Me (Really Love Me)," and forty-seven seconds of Martha Mears singing "My Foolish Heart" from the only movie made from one of his stories.

And then I wrote again:

Fall 1977

Hi Again:

I noticed in one of your stories you had a character talking about how the U.S. and Canada are basically the same. I agree that our lifestyles are very similar, but we are not as outgoing, nationalist, or proud; we might hum our anthem, on a good day. Sometimes I think I can't survive this . . .

And again and again:

Goddamn Useless Conversations, Part IV
December, 1977

Dear Jerry:

Hope you don't mind the informality, but I think I have known you long enough now to qualify for a first-name relationship. I see that you (might have!) had a short story in Esquire, *but there are doubts . . . I am growing hungry for new Salinger material. Will your fans be quenched? Do you have anything more about Holden Caulfield? My own writing is improving, but publication remains elusive. Hope you received my tape of music. I'm still*

*open to your visit anytime. You'd enjoy the Falls in
winter. Grand.*

Cheers,
Michael Clarkson

Salinger did not respond to any of my letters and I was
getting more stressed, feeling more empty and lonely, although Jennifer was a good companion in domestic ways and
a good mother. From *Catcher*, I thought Salinger could help
me because he featured Holden as a catcher in the rye: "What
I have to do, I have to catch everybody if they start to go over
the cliff—I mean if they're running and they don't look where
they're going I have to come out from somewhere and *catch*
them."

On June 13, 1978, I kissed Jennifer, Paul, and Kevin goodbye, strapped myself into a Ford Cortina and headed toward
the United States and New England. There were no Internet
maps or cell phones or Google in those days, just a faded Eastern Seaboard road map from the gas station. My depression
was overcome by adrenaline—I was going to meet J. D. Salinger the person.

Long drives are usually lonely, like the rest of my frig-
gin' life, but I really didn't need music because my internal
orchestra was humming. I was on my way to see an old friend
I'd never met. I tried to picture how he'd look; the only thing
I had to go on was a black-and-white photo from twenty-five
years earlier, the one he yanked off the dust jacket of *Catcher*
because he thought author's personal lives and pictures should
not distract from the message of their stories. I was beginning

to think he'd like me because I was like him. And to hell with the rest of the world.

At the first gas fill-up, just across the border, I cleared the passenger seat of Frito Lay and his books so that he could eventually ride shotgun. I had no idea where we'd go and I didn't have a lot of cash for extras. Maybe we'd start on a sequel to *Catcher*.

Near the Cornish town hall, a woman plucking her garden said he lived "about five miles up the mountain," pointing to a dirt and gravel road. For the next forty-five minutes, I drove up and down that small mountain, with the gravel on the road making a lot of noise, past farmhouses, clearings, homes with no lawns to be tended, a house with an oversized skylight, one dirt road leading to the next over the hills and vales, and people who were friendly enough but about as cooperative as their dairy cows. I wondered who else was hiding what, or whom. There were signs prohibiting hunting and fishing and trespassing, but nothing about stalking.

Nearly forty years later, I don't regret what happened next but I still have mixed feelings about publishing the story. I don't like exploiting people and in a way I think I did. It's complex. After coming home, I felt I also had some obligation to the many fans who got turned away, and indeed to Salinger himself to get this message out. And yet, I still have a leftover feeling of exploitation.

The beacon in my life now is Jennifer, my wife of forty-three years, along with my two sons and two granddaughters. Salinger inspired my prose, although I chose to go into nonfiction. I've had eight books published, mostly on psychology, fear, and stress, and do some professional speaking on the subjects. I hope to help people with their own issues of stress and depression.

In the fashion of the master, I built a wooden fort in my backyard in Fort Erie and go there regularly to write in front of a campfire and wonder where the ducks go in winter.

"A FROZEN MOMENT IN TIME"

INTERVIEW WITH BETTY EPPES
BATON ROUGE SUNDAY ADVOCATE
JUNE 29, 1980

First off, there's no more to Holden Caulfield, so we might as well stop IF-ing about him. It's all in the book if you want to know the truth, all of it. I asked old J.D. and he told me. "Read the book again. It's all there. Holden Caulfield's only a frozen moment in time."

I knew that's what you'd have to know right off or you'd never show J.D. the respect of reading what he had to say and all. It would've been stupid on my part to go all the way up to New England, stand in the middle of the street with J.D. while everybody craned their necks at us, and ask him only one question. Even if it is one that everybody's harped on since the very second *Catcher* appeared. J.D. was pretty nice about it, coming into town to talk to me and all. And since he did create Holden Caulfield and give him to us, the least we can do in return is sit still and take a straight look at the mess that J.D. got himself into by deciding to publish *Catcher*. It's only polite, even if J.D. never let old Holden grow up.

J. D. Salinger stepped out of the covered bridge's shadow-black maw into the white light of mid-morning and headed up Bridge Street to the spot designated in my note of the day before.

No living American writer has captured a larger following than Salinger, short story writer and creator of Holden Caulfield, hero of *The Catcher in the Rye*. His devotees divide into two camps: admirers of his extraordinary writing ability and fans of larger-than-life Caulfield. Both factions are avid, almost rabid seekers of the reason why Salinger ceased publishing and turned his back on them. Finding facts is extremely difficult, as Salinger has lived in self-imposed exile for 27 years. Rarely venturing into public places, he avoids personal interaction and is not willingly photographed.

Walking along the maple-lined street in Windsor, Vt., only his height was what I'd expected. He was 61 and his hair, silver as the too-brilliant morning, jarred. The casualness of his jeans and shirt-jac did not lend itself to our exchange of greetings. His extended hand shook and there was neither warmth nor welcome in his voice as he asked his stock question: "Why did you come here?"

The tension was jam thick and he appeared ready to bolt. Holden Caulfield seemed the safest place to begin.

"There's no more to Holden Caulfield," Salinger explained. "Read the book again. It's all there. Holden Caulfield's only a frozen moment in time."

In the 1953 interview he granted to a student for her high school paper, Salinger answered the question of whether *Catcher* is autobiographical. "Sort of. I was much relieved when I finished it. My boyhood was very much the same as that of the boy in the book. And it was a great relief telling people about it." But on the corner of Windsor Bridge and Main in 1980, Salinger hedged.

"I don't know about Holden anymore. I don't know," he said, nervously shifting his feet and fingering the briefcase under his arm. "I'm sure I must of said that once, but I don't know anymore."

Careful research into Salinger's background and study of *Catcher* reveals screaming similarities: Caulfield is a New Yorker. Jerome David Salinger was born in New York City on Jan. 1, 1919, of an Irish mother and a Jewish father. Caulfield's family is affluent. Salinger grew up in Manhattan with his older sister Doris, enjoying the comforts his father's prosperous meat importing business afforded.

The similarities of their educational background are pronounced. Both Caulfield and Salinger attended public elementary schools, flunked out of at least one prep school, and were interested in writing. Caulfield excelled in English and Salinger was editor of his prep school year book. But Salinger outstripped Caulfield by graduating from Pennsylvania's Valley Forge Military Academy.

Perhaps Salinger is reluctant to now admit *Catcher* is autobiographical because he, unlike Caulfield, grew older.

Salinger attended New York University before a 1937 trip to Poland where he was to learn ham shipping. He did not become involved in the meat business, but the French and German he learned proved invaluable during his military service.

He was drafted into the Army in 1942 and went overseas in the Counter Intelligence Corps. His proficiency in foreign languages proved a valuable tool in ferreting out enemy agents. He took part in the Normandy invasion and returned to America at war's end.

Given Salinger's family background, why writing instead of commerce?

"I can't say exactly why I became a writer," Salinger said. "It's different for each person." Pressed on the point of whether it was a conscious decision, he shook his head and gazed up into the green mountains of Vermont. "I don't know, I don't know."

But write he did.

He took Whit Burnett's 1939 short story course at Columbia and before being drafted, had stories published in *Collier's, The Saturday Evening Post,* and *Esquire.* In 1941, though it was not published for five years, his short story introducing Holden Caulfield was sold to *The New Yorker.* This work established him as a writer of exceptional ability. The 1951 publication of *Catcher* brought phenomenal recognition and publicity. Then J. D. Salinger turned and walked away.

He talked of his reasons for living in isolation. "I could not have forseen all that's happened since I began this writing business," he said, "and sometime I almost wish I'd never published." To the question of future publishing plans, Salinger replied, "I have absolutely no plans to publish at this time." His stance was uneasy and his speech impatient. "All I want now is to write and to be left absolutely alone."

Catcher still sells at a rate of 400,000 copies annually, and two of every three adolescents who read it perceive Salinger as an all-seeing guru. They yearn for further word from him and speculate on what Holden Caulfield would be like if he grew up. And over the three decades since *Catcher* appeared, Salinger's legend has ballooned into myth.

And Salinger remains a mystery. Living in his large chalet-type house perched high on a nearly inaccessible cliff in remote Cornish, N.H., he rarely speaks with outsiders. A clue may lie in the rumor that Salinger is interested in eastern religion. Some of his work dealing with the fictional Glass family is definitely experimental, and his comments on subject and theme were pure Zen.

"There's so much that cannot be known," he said. "We each have to find our own way. We make decisions along the way, of course, but the subject may choose the writer."

In 1955 he married former Radcliffe student Claire Douglas. Now divorced, they have two children—Margaret Ann, now 24, and Matthew, 20. Despite his seclusion, Salinger has a close circle of friends and relatives. Some acquaintances commented on J. D. Salinger—the man, not the myth.

"He's a really nice person," a Windsor specialty shop owner said, "as long as you let him speak first. You can't approach him. You have to let him make the first move. Just because he says something to you one day doesn't mean he'll do the same the next. And anybody who doesn't deal with him in this way is asking to be snubbed."

"Did you see him?" A teenage boy on the street near the post office where Salinger went for his mail asked. "He parked on the New Hampshire side of the covered bridge. It's closed and he saved seven miles of driving by walking from there to the post office. You can see he's fit enough to walk it. I'm fat compared to him and anybody can see I'm not fat. I sure admire a man that keeps in shape."

"Yes, he's a friend of mine," a neighbor said, "and I keep him that way by never, never bringing up his writing to him. He talks to me about it from time to time,

of course, and I'm always willing to hear what he's willing to say and a lot more. But I've learned you can't ask Mr. Salinger questions. He doesn't want to be bothered."

And in nearby Claremont, N.H., the owner of a bookstore Salinger visits infrequently shared her observations of him. "He's such a peculiar man, not like any customer you ever saw. He'll come in and doesn't want you to speak even. And if you ask if he needs help, he just shakes his head and walks away to look. If he's ever bought anything, and he may possible have, I don't recall it. One day my little girl was here with me when he came in. She was so delighted. She got a copy of a book of his and went over and asked for his autograph. He told her curtly that he didn't give autographs and turned on his heel and walked out. He is a peculiar man."

Salinger's refusal to sign autographs has confounded his admirers for three decades.

"I don't do it," he explained. "It's a meaningless gesture. It's all right for actors and actresses, people with only their faces and names to give. But it's different with writers. They give their work. Signing autographs doesn't mean anything. It's cheap and I will not do it!"

Salinger says he is becoming embittered. "I'm tired of being collared in elevators, stopped on the street, and of interlopers on my private property. I've made my position clear for 30 years," he insisted, squinting his bright-dark eyes and beetling his brows. "I want to be left alone, absolutely. Why can't my life be my own?"

He turned away but stopped to answer whether or not he's still writing.

"Yes I am," he said. "I told you, I love to write and I assure you I write regularly. But I write for myself. For my own pleasure. And I want to be left alone to do it."

With those words he walked off down Bridge Street to the covered bridge. Watching his tall agile figure disappear into the shadows, questions floated up in my mind. If J. D. Salinger is sincere in his desire for the hermit's life, why come nine miles to talk with an absolute stranger? Could it be that he wants to be remembered and read, but isn't willing to pay the price for remembrance? Rethinking our encounter, I must turn Salinger's stock question back on him—J.D., why did you come?

Old Holden would be the first to understand that to have absolute privacy, all doors must remain absolutely closed.

THE LAST INTERVIEW

DEPOSITION OF PLAINTIFF JEROME D. SALINGER,
TAKEN BY DEFENDANTS, PURSUANT TO NOTICE, AT
THE OFFICE OF MESSRS. SATTERLEE & STEPHENS,
230 PARK AVENUE, NEW YORK, N.Y., 10169, ON
OCT. 7, 1986, AT 2:10 P.M., BEFORE DONNA ROGERS,
A SHORTHAND REPORTER AND NOTARY PUBLIC OF
THE STATE OF NEW YORK.

In the early 1980s, the English critic and biographer Ian Hamilton set out to write the first full-scale biography of Salinger. Hamilton secured a $100,000 advance from Random House and wrote Salinger asking for cooperation. In his reply, Salinger slammed the door and nailed it shut:

It has always been a most terrible and almost unassimilable wonder to me that it is evidently quite lawful, the world over, for a newspaper or a publishing house to "commission" somebody, in the not particularly fair name of good journalism or basic profitable academic research, to break into the privacy not only of a person not reasonably suspected of criminal activity but into the lives as well, however glancingly, of that person's relatives and friends. I've despaired long ago of finding any justice in the common practice. Let alone any goodness or decency.

Hamilton oddly interpreted this raw plea—almost a shriek of pain—as a come-on. He showed the letter to a literary friend, who said, "I can't stop you," meant, "Please go ahead."

A bigger blunder came when the biographer quoted from troves of Salinger letters he found in various archives. The letters were vivid. When Salinger lost his sweetie Oona O'Neill to the much older Charlie Chaplin, he described the actor "squatting grey and nude" on a chest of drawers, "swinging his thyroid around his head by his bamboo cane, like a dead rat. Oona in an aquamarine gown, applauding madly from the bathroom." When Salinger saw the pre-publication galleys of *J. D. Salinger: A Writing Life*, he threatened to sue for copyright infringement.

Hamilton produced another draft of the book with Salinger's best lines paraphrased. The rewrite didn't help and Salinger filed suit. He said he was "utterly dismayed" to find "the core" of the book was in his own words, and that any paraphrasing by Hamilton was merely "a few cosmetic changes." The book was delayed while the court case proceeded. Hamilton figured the author was bluffing:

> Sooner or later, if Salinger did persevere, he would be obliged to make a personal appearance—in either a courtroom or in the offices of the Random House attorneys. He would be required, at the very least, to give a deposition. That is to say, an interview. And as we knew all too well, this man didn't give interviews.

Except he did.

Robert Callagy of the distinguished firm Satterlee & Stephens, which once represented Mark Twain, was the lawyer for Random House and Hamilton. Callagy told *New York* magazine that the 68-year-old Salinger was remarkably well-preserved though somewhat deaf. "He is graying, with stark features. He is well-dressed, and appears quite athletic. He comes across more as a businessman than an author. He sort of objected to the fact that he had to be questioned at all."

Sort of? No kidding.

●

CALLAGY: Would you please state your name and address for the record.

SALINGER: Jerome D. Salinger, Lang Road, Cornish, New Hampshire 03745.

CALLAGY: Mr. Salinger, how long have you lived in Cornish, New Hampshire?

SALINGER: About thirty years.

CALLAGY: Are you currently employed?

SALINGER: No, I'm not employed.

CALLAGY: Do you own shares in any corporation—

SALINGER: No.

MARCIA PAUL [**SALINGER**'s *lawyer*]: Mr. Salinger, why don't you wait until he finishes the question? I don't know that Mr. Callagy had completed his question.

SALINGER: He dropped his voice. [*to* **CALLAGY**] Yes.

CALLAGY: Do you have any interests in any partnership which owns rights in any of your literary works?

SALINGER: No.

CALLAGY: Who do you currently live with in your home in Cornish?

PAUL: I am going to object to that question on the grounds of relevance.

CALLAGY: What I would like to establish is whether Mr. Salinger is the copyright owner of certain works or whether he may have transferred rights to his wife or children or what have you, and so that was the purpose of that question.

PAUL: I would appreciate it if you would withdraw your last question and come back to it if you feel you need it at the conclusion of this line of questioning.

CALLAGY: All right. [*to* **SALINGER**] Mr. Salinger, when was the last time that you wrote any work of fiction for publication?

SALINGER: I'm not sure exactly.

CALLAGY: At any time during the past twenty years, have you written a work of fiction for publication?

SALINGER: That has been published, you mean?

CALLAGY: That has been published.

SALINGER: No.

CALLAGY: At any time during the past twenty years, have you written a work of nonfiction for publication?

SALINGER: No, I have not.

CALLAGY: At any time during the past twenty years, have you written any fiction which has not been published?

SALINGER: Yes.

CALLAGY: Could you describe for me what works of fiction you have written which has not been published?

PAUL: You are talking about a general description?

CALLAGY: Yes.

SALINGER: It would be very difficult to do. Work of fiction as I've always written fiction.

CALLAGY: Have you written any full-length works of fiction during the past twenty years which have not been published?

SALINGER: Could you frame that in a different way. What do you mean by a full-length work? You mean ready for publication?

CALLAGY: As opposed to a short story or a fictional piece or a magazine submission.

SALINGER: It's very difficult to answer. I don't write that way. I just start writing fiction and see what happens to it.

CALLAGY: Maybe an easier way to approach this is, would you tell me what your literary efforts have been in the field of fiction within the last twenty years?

SALINGER: Could I tell you or would I tell you?

PAUL: Sir, if you can answer the question, please try to answer the question in a general fashion. I think Mr. Callagy is trying to inquire generally what you have been working on in the last twenty years.

SALINGER: Just a work of fiction. That's all. That's the only description I can really give it.

CALLAGY: When you say "a work of fiction," are you talking about a single work as opposed to multiple works of fiction?

SALINGER: That too is subject to much thought. I couldn't give you a direct answer to that. It's a long piece of fiction, and that describes it best.

CALLAGY: Is that piece of fiction in manuscript form at this time?

SALINGER: As opposed to what?

CALLAGY: As opposed to in bits and pieces of paper that may be in various states of completion.

PAUL: I object to the form of the question. [*to* **SALINGER**] If you understand it, you can answer it.

SALINGER: It's very difficult to answer it. The answer is really in both forms.

CALLAGY: Am I to understand that in the past twenty years you have worked and have prepared a work of fiction which has not been published as opposed to multiple works?

SALINGER: I don't think that could be said. It's very hard to define. It's almost impossible to define. I work with characters and as they develop, I just go on from there.

CALLAGY: In the past twenty years, have you entered into any contracts with any publishers—

SALINGER: No.

CALLAGY: —with respect to any work that you would write—

SALINGER: No.

CALLAGY: Have you entered into any agreements with any magazine respecting any work that you would write—

SALINGER: No.

PAUL: Can you please, Mr. Salinger, wait until he finishes the question before answering it?

SALINGER: Sorry.

CALLAGY: Have you during the past twenty years written any short stories for publication?

SALINGER: No.

CALLAGY: Do you know an individual by the name of Ian Hamilton?

SALINGER: Know of him? Know of him?

CALLAGY: Yes.

SALINGER: I know of him, yes.

CALLAGY: When did you first become aware of Mr. Hamilton?

SALINGER: About three years ago, actually.

CALLAGY: Can you tell me the circumstances under which you became aware of him?

SALINGER: Yes.

CALLAGY: Would you tell me, please?

SALINGER: Yes. He wrote and told me that Random House had commissioned him to write a biography of me, and more than that, I can't say offhand; I don't remember.

CALLAGY: Did you ever speak to him on the telephone?

SALINGER: No, I have not.

CALLAGY: Did you ever speak to anyone about him with the exception of counsel?

SALINGER: I may have. To my agent, yes.

CALLAGY: Other than your agent, have you ever spoken to anyone about Mr. Hamilton?

SALINGER: Yes, I'd say so.

CALLAGY: With respect to your agent, who at your agency, and I assume you mean your literary agent, the Ober agency, who at that agency did you speak to about Mr. Hamilton?

PAUL: Let the record reflect that Mr. Salinger nodded his head in response to Mr. Callagy's statement that he assumes he meant at his literary agency.

SALINGER: I'm sorry.

CALLAGY: Who was it at the Ober agency that you spoke to about Mr. Hamilton?

SALINGER: Dorothy Olding.

CALLAGY: When did you for the first time speak to Ms. Olding about Mr. Hamilton?

SALINGER: I don't remember.

CALLAGY: What was the substance of that discussion?

SALINGER: I assume I told her that—the contents of Hamilton's letter.

CALLAGY: Anything else that you recall?

SALINGER: Not that I recall.

CALLAGY: You also indicated that you have spoken to others about Mr. Hamilton. Who have you spoken to about Mr. Hamilton?

SALINGER: It's very hard to answer. It's almost anybody who's heard that this thing is in procedure would ask me about it. But offhand, I can't think of any names.

CALLAGY: Have you sent any letters to anyone regarding the biography which Mr. Hamilton was writing?

SALINGER: I don't think so.

PAUL: Answer to the best of your recollection. I was just trying to indicate to you to wait until Mr. Callagy finishes his question before answering.

SALINGER: I see.

CALLAGY: Have you been aware that certain acquaintances of yours were cooperating with Mr. Hamilton in connection with the writing of the biography?

PAUL: I object to the form of the question. [*to* **SALINGER**] You can just go ahead and answer it. I am just objecting for the record.

SALINGER: Only if those acquaintances wrote and told me so.

CALLAGY: Did you receive any such letters?

SALINGER: Yes, I have.

CALLAGY: From whom did you receive the letters?

SALINGER: My son, for one; some Army acquaintances; I believe my sister: I believe my daughter wrote to me about it. Other names I can't recall offhand.

CALLAGY: Do you have the letters you received from your son, from the Army acquaintances, from your sister, and from your daughter?

SALINGER: I believe I have some.

CALLAGY: Do you have those with you today?

PAUL: May I respond to that? We have letters in our office. I did not understand them to be within the scope of the request that accompanied this notice of deposition. I have no problem whatsoever with producing them and will do so. We just don't have the letters with us at the moment.

CALLAGY: I understand. [*to* **SALINGER**] Did you respond to these letters in writing?

SALINGER: I may have to one or two.

CALLAGY: Did you retain a copy of your responses to these letters?

SALINGER: I'm not sure.

CALLAGY: Do you recall to whom you may have responded in writing?

SALINGER: No, I don't, offhand.

CALLAGY: I will direct this request to your counsel. To the extent that Mr. Salinger has retained copies of his responses to various of the letters he received regarding Mr. Hamilton's biography, I would ask for their production.

PAUL: We will attempt to determine if any such documents are in existence and within the possession, custody, and control of this witness. If so, will promptly advise you as to whether or not they are and take under advisement the request for their production.

CALLAGY: Mr. Salinger, do you recall in the letters that you did send by way of response, what you said?

SALINGER: No, I don't think I do exactly.

CALLAGY: Did you encourage these people to cooperate with Mr. Hamilton?

SALINGER: No.

CALLAGY: Did you encourage or did you discourage them from cooperating with Mr. Hamilton?

SALINGER: It was usually after the fact, they had told me what they had done or not done.

CALLAGY: Do you recall what, if anything, you said to them in this regard?

SALINGER: No, I can't at the moment.

CALLAGY: I would ask the court reporter to mark as the first exhibit a letter which is undated from Mr. Salinger to Ian Hamilton but which is attached to a letter from Harold Ober Associates to Robert L. Bernstein dated August 4, 1983.

> [*Letter, undated, from Mr. Salinger to Ian Hamilton attached to a letter from Harold Ober Associates to Robert L. Bernstein dated Aug. 4, 1983, marked* Defendants' Exhibit A *for identification, as of this date.*]

CALLAGY: Mr. Salinger, I show you what's been marked *Exhibit A*, and I ask you if you received a copy of the first letter which forms that exhibit from Dorothy Olding.

PAUL: Do you understand the question, Mr. Salinger? Just this first page you're referring to?

SALINGER: I'm not sure I do understand your question. What is the question?

PAUL: Did you receive a copy—excuse me Mr. Callagy, if I may—did you receive a copy of this first page of this exhibit?

SALINGER: No, I did not.

CALLAGY: In or about August of 1983, did you ask your literary agent to contact Random House regarding the forthcoming Hamilton biography?

SALINGER: No, I don't recall doing so.

CALLAGY: When was the first time that you became aware that Dorothy Olding of Harold Ober Associates had written to Random House, if you ever did?

SALINGER: I don't think I ever did. I'm not sure. I'm not aware of this letter at all.

CALLAGY: Is today the first time that you have seen the first page of Exhibit A?

SALINGER: Yes, it is.

CALLAGY: Going to the second page of Exhibit A, which is a letter to Ian Hamilton, did you prepare that letter?

SALINGER: Yes.

CALLAGY: Did you send it to Mr. Hamilton?

SALINGER: Yes.

CALLAGY: Do you recall when you sent it to Mr. Hamilton?

SALINGER: No. There's no date on that. How is it there's no date on it?

PAUL: You can't ask Mr. Callagy a question. There doesn't appear to be a date on it. Mr. Callagy has asked you if you know the date.

SALINGER: I don't know. The only reason I asked it—

CALLAGY: So by reference to the letter and to the first page of Exhibit A, does that refresh your recollection as to when you may have sent the letter to—

SALINGER: I'm afraid not.

CALLAGY: —Mr. Hamilton?

SALINGER: No, it doesn't.

CALLAGY: Have you ever had any discussions with anyone from Random House regarding this biography?

SALINGER: No.

CALLAGY: Have you ever had any discussions with anyone from Harold Ober Associates regarding the biography?

SALINGER: Yes.

CALLAGY: When was the first time you had any discussions with anyone from that literary agency regarding the biography?

SALINGER: I believe when I first heard from Hamilton.

CALLAGY: Can you place that in time?

SALINGER: No. Shortly after I received his letter.

CALLAGY: So that would be sometime prior to August of 1983?

SALINGER: I don't know, really. I should think so.

CALLAGY: Do you recall whether you had a telephone conference or a meeting with someone from your literary agency regarding this subject?

SALINGER: I believe it would have been over the telephone.

CALLAGY: Do you recall with whom you spoke?

SALINGER: It would almost certainly be Dorothy Olding.

CALLAGY: Do you recall the substance of the conversation?

SALINGER: No, I do not.

CALLAGY: Did you make any notes of the conversation?

SALINGER: No, I did not.

CALLAGY: How many conversations did you have with Dorothy Olding regarding the biography?

SALINGER: I don't know.

CALLAGY: Would all of these conversations have been on the telephone?

SALINGER: Yes.

CALLAGY: Did you speak to anyone other than Dorothy Olding at Harold Ober Associates regarding the biography?

SALINGER: At Harold Ober Associates?

CALLAGY: Correct.

SALINGER: No.

CALLAGY: Do you have any recollection of the substance of any of the conversations that you had with Dorothy Olding regarding the biography?

SALINGER: No, I don't think I do.

CALLAGY: Did there come a point in time when you became aware that a bound galley existed for the biography?

SALINGER: A point in time?

CALLAGY: Yes.

PAUL: Did there come a point in time I think was the question. Did there come a point in time in which you learned?

SALINGER: Yes, I suppose so.

CALLAGY: Do you recall when that was?

SALINGER: No, I don't.

CALLAGY: I would ask the reporter to mark as the next exhibit a bound galley entitled "Uncorrected Proof, J. D. Salinger: A Writing Life by Ian Hamilton."

PAUL: At this time, I would like to request that Exhibit B be marked confidential and under seal.

CALLAGY: That's agreeable.

[*Bound galley entitled "Uncorrected Proof, J. D.
Salinger: A Writing Life by Ian Hamilton" marked*
Defendants' Exhibit B *for identification, as of this
date.*]

CALLAGY: Mr. Salinger, I show you what has been marked as
Defendants' Exhibit B for identification and I ask you if you
have ever seen that document before.

SALINGER: What document?

CALLAGY: What you have in your hands.

PAUL: In this form, Mr. Callagy?

CALLAGY: That's correct.

SALINGER: No, I've never see it in this form.

CALLAGY: Directing your attention to Exhibit B and specifically the third page from the beginning of that exhibit, have
you seen that page and the balance of the exhibit before?

SALINGER: I'm not sure—

PAUL: He is talking about from here forward, from the third
page.

SALINGER: What is the question?

CALLAGY: Have you ever seen that before?

SALINGER: I don't know if I've seen the exact same thing but something quite like it. Probably the same thing. I don't know.

CALLAGY: When did you see that for the first time?

SALINGER: I don't know exactly when I received it.

CALLAGY: From whom did you receive it?

SALINGER: My agent, Dorothy Olding, sent it to me.

CALLAGY: Did she send it to you with a letter?

SALINGER: She sent it to me in the mail.

CALLAGY: Did a letter accompany the document that she sent you?

SALINGER: There was a note attached but I don't remember what it said. Something personal.

CALLAGY: Did you keep that note?

SALINGER: I don't—no, I don't think so.

CALLAGY: When did you receive it?

SALINGER: I can't tell you that. I don't know. You mean the exact date, I take it?

CALLAGY: Yes.

SALINGER: No, I don't know.

CALLAGY: Did Dorothy tell you where she had received it?

SALINGER: She said she received it from a friend.

CALLAGY: What did you do with the copy you received?

SALINGER: Copy of what?

CALLAGY: What did you do with what you received from Dorothy Olding?

SALINGER: The—galley proofs or—

CALLAGY: Yes.

SALINGER: I kept them.

CALLAGY: Do you still have it?

SALINGER: I believe so.

CALLAGY: Did you read it?

SALINGER: Yes.

CALLAGY: Did you read it from cover to cover?

SALINGER: Yes.

CALLAGY: You are sure that at the time you received the galley, it had no cover on it similar to Exhibit B?

SALINGER: Yes—

PAUL: You said yes. Yes, you are sure that it did not have a cover?

SALINGER: I believe so.

CALLAGY: Do you know if what you received was a photocopy or was it similar to Exhibit B, which appears to be a printer's proof?

SALINGER: That, I don't know.

CALLAGY: Where is the document that you received from Dorothy Olding?

SALINGER: Home, at my home.

CALLAGY: Did you make any notes or markings on those proofs when you received them?

SALINGER: I may have underlined some things.

CALLAGY: Do you know what you underlined?

SALINGER: No, I don't.

CALLAGY: Do you know the purpose for which you made those underlinings?

SALINGER: No, I don't offhand remember.

CALLAGY: Did you discuss these proofs with anyone?

PAUL: Other than his attorneys?

CALLAGY: Other than counsel.

SALINGER: Other than my attorneys?

CALLAGY: Right.

SALINGER: No, surely not.

CALLAGY: How many times did you read these proofs that you received from Dorothy Olding?

SALINGER: How many times did I receive—

PAUL: Did you read them.

SALINGER: Once was adequate.

PAUL: Off the record.

[*Discussion off the record.*]

CALLAGY: Did you send any letter to Dorothy Olding regarding the proofs that you read?

SALINGER: I don't—I don't remember.

CALLAGY: Directing your attention to the cover of what's been marked as *Exhibit B* and specifically the legend that says, and I quote, "Since these are uncorrected proofs, please do not quote for publication until you check your copy against the finished book."
     Have you ever seen that legend before today?

SALINGER: No.

CALLAGY: Do you know whether or not that legend was on the page proofs that you say [you] received?

SALINGER: I don't remember seeing it.

CALLAGY: I would ask for production of the page proofs that the witness received and currently has at his home in New Hampshire.

PAUL: We'll take it under advisement.

CALLAGY: Do you have any recollection as to what notes or markings you may have put on the page proofs that you received?

SALINGER: No.

PAUL: I believe the witness has already testified that he may have underscored some items in the page proofs. I assume your question was other than his previous testimony.

CALLAGY: That's right. [*to* **SALINGER**] Did you prepare any notes at the time you read the page proofs that you had received from Dorothy Olding?

SALINGER: No.

CALLAGY: I previously asked you whether or not you discussed with anyone other than counsel the page proofs that you read, and your answer was no?

SALINGER: No.

CALLAGY: Did you prepare any comparisons based on what you read in the page proofs that you received with any letters or other writings of yours?

PAUL: Are you asking him at any time whether he prepared any such comparisons, or at the time he received the—

CALLAGY: We will break it down—

PAUL: —page proofs—

CALLAGY: We will start with, at the time you received the page proofs, did you prepare any comparisons comparing what you read in the printed galleys with any of your writings?

SALINGER: Say that again.

[*Question read.*]

SALINGER: What do you mean by "prepare"?

CALLAGY: Did you make any comparisons in written form?

SALINGER: No.

CALLAGY: Have you ever made any comparisons in written form comparing what you read in the galleys which you received from Dorothy Olding with any of your writings?

PAUL: Mr. Callagy, you know that there was an exhibit annexed to his affidavit—

CALLAGY: I want to know if he prepared it.

PAUL: By "prepared," do you mean if he wrote it out by hand or did he participate in any way in its preparation—

CALLAGY: Let's start out with whether or not the witness wrote it out by hand.

SALINGER: Wrote out what by hand?

PAUL: The exhibit to your affidavit is what Mr. Callagy is referring to, which compares your letters with what is in the page proofs.

SALINGER: No.

CALLAGY: Let me mark as the next exhibit—and we can do this with the same stipulation of confidentiality—Exhibit C, which is a textual comparison of certain of Mr. Salinger's letters with Mr. Hamilton's biography. I would like to mark that with the understanding this document will be under confidentiality treatment.

PAUL: And seal. I would like the record to reflect that your description of the document is accurate but there may be a discrepancy to the extent you are questioning the witness with respect to the revised page proofs which are Exhibit B and the comparative material in what is now Exhibit C, which as I understand it is—actually, I withdraw that. I don't know which this is.

>   [*Textual comparison of certain of Mr. Salinger's
>   letters with Mr. Hamilton's biography marked*
>   Defendants' Exhibit C *for identification, as of
>   this date.*]

CALLAGY: Mr. Salinger, I show you what's been marked as *Exhibit C*, which is a comparison of certain of your letters with the proofs of the Hamilton biography, and I ask you, did you prepare that document yourself?

SALINGER: Prepare this piece of writing?

CALLAGY: That's right.

SALINGER: No.

CALLAGY: Do you know who prepared it?

SALINGER: Do I know who prepared it? I presume it was prepared by my lawyers.

CALLAGY: Prior to the time that document was submitted to court, did you ever see it?

SALINGER: No.
    Oh, yes, this one. Sorry. I have seen this one.

PAUL: The witness's recollection will stand but I don't want the record to be inaccurate. That is a document which was annexed to your affidavit, Mr. Salinger.

SALINGER: Yes, that's the one. I thought you meant the timing—

CALLAGY: Did you prepare any document that was similar to Exhibit C with respect to the galleys that you received from Dorothy Olding?

SALINGER: Prepare? No, I did not prepare anything.

PAUL: I am somewhat confused at this point and perhaps the record is correct and I am not. But these unrevised proofs—is this, Exhibit B, what was produced two or three weeks ago, or is this the May galleys?

CALLAGY: No. This is the May galleys.

PAUL: The problem that I am having is that in our papers, we just happened to refer to the May galleys as May galleys and the revised page proofs as the second version of the book.

What is Exhibit B is the first version of the book, which was produced sometime in May, is that correct?

CALLAGY: Why don't we refer to Exhibit B, for your convenience, as the May galleys.

PAUL: Okay. [*to* **SALINGER**] Mr. Salinger, did you understand that what is Exhibit B is the material that you received in May?

SALINGER: I'm not sure I did.

CALLAGY: Let me ask the witness. [*to* **SALINGER**] In May of 1986 or thereabouts, did you receive certain documents from your literary agent, Dorothy Olding?

SALINGER: Yes.

CALLAGY: Were those what we'll call the May galleys for the Hamilton biography?

SALINGER: I don't recall what they were called but this I can tell you, they looked like galley proofs. That's all I can tell you. I've seen galley proofs many times in my life, and that's what they looked like to me.

CALLAGY: Did you read those galley proofs at the time you received them?

SALINGER: Yes, I did, I did.

CALLAGY: What did you do with those galley proofs?

SALINGER: I kept them.

CALLAGY: Do you currently have those galley proofs in New Hampshire?

SALINGER: I believe so.

CALLAGY: Were those the galley proofs that you made some markings on?

SALINGER: When I read anything, I have a pencil in hand, that's all I can tell you, and I usually mark something that impresses me one way or another. Past that point, I don't know what to tell you about them.

CALLAGY: When you say you mark something that impresses you, when you use those terms, are you talking about inter-lineations or are you talking about inclusion of [words]?

SALINGER: Possibly I mean it in many senses. I'm a writer.

CALLAGY: Do you recall for what purpose you made any markings on those galley proofs?

SALINGER: No, I can't recall whether I made it for any purpose.

CALLAGY: Did you ever show those markings to anyone?

SALINGER: I don't think so, no.

CALLAGY: Have you ever shown that galley to anyone?

SALINGER: Galley as itself?

CALLAGY: The one you have at home.

SALINGER: You mean give it to somebody to read?

CALLAGY: Right.

SALINGER: No.

CALLAGY: Other than your counsel, have you ever discussed that galley with anyone?

SALINGER: Interested friends.

CALLAGY: Who would those interested friends be?

PAUL: Could we go off the record for a moment?

CALLAGY: Yes.

   [*Discussion off the record.*]

SALINGER: My sister; my son; my daughter.
   I can't see the relevancy of this. I don't like to bring people's names into this.

CALLAGY: Is that all?

PAUL: If there's somebody else who comes to mind with whom you discussed—the galleys we're now talking about?

CALLAGY: Yes.

PAUL: —the May galleys.

SALINGER: No, nobody else comes to mind.

CALLAGY: What did you say to your sister about the galleys?

SALINGER: I don't remember exactly what I said to her.

CALLAGY: Did you tell her that you objected to any portion of the galleys that you had read?

SALINGER: To any portion of the galleys?

CALLAGY: Yes.

SALINGER: No.

CALLAGY: Did you tell her that you had objected in any way to the galleys?

SALINGER: Yes.

CALLAGY: What did you tell her?

SALINGER: I don't remember what I told her. I made it clear that I objected.

CALLAGY: Do you recall what you said in that regard?

SALINGER: Say that again.

CALLAGY: Do you recall what you said in that regard?

SALINGER: No, I don't.

CALLAGY: Was your conversation with your sister in person or over the telephone?

SALINGER: Was it what?

CALLAGY: In person or over the telephone?

SALINGER: Over the telephone.

CALLAGY: How many conversations did you have with her on that subject?

SALINGER: One, as far as I remember.

CALLAGY: Was that conversation at or about the time that you had reviewed what we've called the May galleys?

SALINGER: Say that again.

CALLAGY: Was that conversation with your sister at or about the time you had reviewed the May galleys?

SALINGER: I can't say. I think probably, yes.

CALLAGY: How about your son? Did you have a conversation with him on the subject of the May galleys?

SALINGER: Yes.

CALLAGY: What did you say to him about the May galleys?

SALINGER: Just that I had received them.

CALLAGY: Anything else?

SALINGER: That I didn't approve or like what I saw.

CALLAGY: Did you tell him in what way you didn't approve?

SALINGER: No, I did not.

CALLAGY: Did you tell him in what way you didn't like the biography?

SALINGER: I didn't go into any detail with him.

CALLAGY: How many conversations did you have with your son in that regard?

SALINGER: I don't remember.

CALLAGY: More than one?

SALINGER: I don't think so.

CALLAGY: Did you send him a copy of the galleys?

SALINGER: No.

CALLAGY: Did you send your sister a copy of the galleys?

SALINGER: No.

CALLAGY: Did you send your sister any letter regarding the galleys?

SALINGER: No.

CALLAGY: Did you send your son any letter regarding the galleys?

SALINGER: No.

CALLAGY: With respect to your daughter, you have told us that you had a conversation with her about the galleys. What did you say to your daughter about the galleys?

SALINGER: Just that I had received them.

CALLAGY: Did you say whether you objected to the galleys?

SALINGER: I must have said the same thing I said to my son.

CALLAGY: Did you say the same thing to your sister that you had said to your son as well?

SALINGER: As far as I can remember.

CALLAGY: At the time you received the galleys, did you become aware that certain correspondence that you had written earlier in your life was referred to?

SALINGER: At the time I received, was I aware of what?

CALLAGY: Were you aware that certain correspondence that you had written earlier in your life was referred to in the galleys?

SALINGER: Not before I received the galleys, no.

PAUL: He said at the time you received them.

SALINGER: At the time I received them what?

PAUL: Did you become aware that certain correspondence that you had written was included in the galleys?

SALINGER: Well, I read the galleys and that was made clear.

CALLAGY: Was that the first time that you had become aware of the existence of this correspondence?

SALINGER: The fact that I had written these letters at all, you mean?

CALLAGY: Well, the fact that the correspondence existed.

SALINGER: It was very dim, if I remembered it at all. The letters were written so long ago it was not clear. I just read them here and that's it.

CALLAGY: When you had this conversation with your sister, did you refer in any way to the correspondence that was referred to in the galleys?

PAUL: I will object to the form of the question.

CALLAGY: When you had this conversation with your sister, did the subject of your correspondence come up?

SALINGER: I don't remember that it did.

CALLAGY: Did the subject of how you were portrayed in the biography come up?

SALINGER: No, not that I remember.

CALLAGY: When you had this conversation with your son, did the subject of correspondence that you had written come up?

SALINGER: No, not that I remember.

CALLAGY: Did the subject of how you were portrayed in the biography come up?

SALINGER: No.

CALLAGY: When you had this conversation with your daughter, did the subject of the correspondence which was referred to in the biography come up?

SALINGER: No. The conversation was similar as it was with my son and daughter.

CALLAGY: All you can recall today is that you said that you objected to the biography?

SALINGER: I said that I didn't like or approve the idea of this.

CALLAGY: Why didn't you like the biography?

SALINGER: Why didn't I like the biography?

CALLAGY: Yes.

SALINGER: It was unauthorized and—not that it was un-authorized. It was full of—in my own reading of the biography?

CALLAGY: Yes.

SALINGER: It was an appropriation of my letters, my personal letters.

CALLAGY: You told us that you told your son that you didn't like it and I asked you in what respect you didn't like it and you have just told us about correspondence.

Was there anything else that you didn't like about the biography other than—

SALINGER: That I mentioned to my son, you mean?

CALLAGY: Yes.

SALINGER: No, I don't think so.

CALLAGY: How about your sister?

SALINGER: I don't think so.

CALLAGY: How about to your daughter?

SALINGER: I don't think so.

CALLAGY: Do you recall when you had this conversation with your son that you in fact referred to the correspondence that had been referred to or quoted in the biography?

SALINGER: I'm not sure of that. I'm not sure.

CALLAGY: Back in 1983, Mr. Hamilton had written to you telling you that he was writing this biography, didn't he, and he asked—

PAUL: Was that a yes in response to his question?

SALINGER: Well, he just showed me the letter, yes.

PAUL: Mr. Salinger, you can't nod your head. The court reporter has to take down—

SALINGER: All right, I'll try.

CALLAGY: He asked to interview you at that time, didn't he?

SALINGER: As far as I remember. I'm not sure. Something about that, yes.

CALLAGY: And you declined to permit him to interview you?

SALINGER: Yes.

CALLAGY: Why did you do that?

SALINGER: Why did I do it?

CALLAGY: Yes.

SALINGER: Because I preferred not to have any book at that time done.

CALLAGY: Have other people in the last twenty-five years asked you for an interview?

SALINGER: Oh, yes.

CALLAGY: Have you ever granted an interview to anyone?

SALINGER: Knowledgeably? No.

CALLAGY: Have you ever granted an interview unknowledgeably to anyone?

SALINGER: Apparently, yes.

CALLAGY: To whom have you granted such interviews?

PAUL: Excuse me. I would like to go off the record here for purposes of determining whether I want to ask that this portion of the record be marked sealed. I would to confer with my client before proceeding.

[*Discussion off the record.*]

PAUL: Mr. Salinger will answer the question but pursuant to our agreement. The answer to this question and any follow-up questions that Mr. Callagy may ask on this particular topic will be deemed confidential and under seal pursuant to the court's instruction.

CALLAGY: Have you ever authorized a biography of yourself?

SALINGER: No.

CALLAGY: Have you ever been requested to authorize a biography of yourself?

SALINGER: Yes.

CALLAGY: Have you received letters containing such requests?

SALINGER: I think so, yes.

CALLAGY: Did you retain those letters?

SALINGER: I don't know. Something may be in my files. I don't know.

CALLAGY: Did you respond to the letters?

SALINGER: Did I respond?

CALLAGY: Yes.

SALINGER: Usually they were sent down to my agent, copies of the letters. Most requests of that kind would go through my agent normally.

CALLAGY: Again, when you say "agent," you are referring to Harold Ober Associates?

SALINGER: Specifically Dorothy Olding.

CALLAGY: How long have you been agented by Harold Ober Associates?

SALINGER: For forty-five years.

CALLAGY: Does Harold Ober Associates serve your interests pursuant to a written agreement? Do they represent you as agent pursuant to a written agreement?

SALINGER: Yes, they do.

CALLAGY: Do you recall when you first entered into a written agreement with Harold Ober Associates?

SALINGER: I don't think I've ever had a written agreement with Harold Ober Associates.

CALLAGY: You don't have a written agreement with them now?

SALINGER: No. They just—an affair of honor, really. They just represent me.

CALLAGY: Have you, during the time that you have been represented by Harold Ober Associates, had the services of any other literary agent in the United States?

SALINGER: No.

CALLAGY: Does Harold Ober Associates collect any royalties that may be due you on account of any works that you have previously published?

SALINGER: All the royalties go through their office.

CALLAGY: With respect to all previously published works, are you the copyright owner, to your knowledge, of the works that you have authored and published?

SALINGER: To my knowledge, yes.

CALLAGY: Have you ever granted a copyright interest in any of your works to any person other than yourself?

SALINGER: To my knowledge, no.

CALLAGY: Have you ever conveyed any copyright interest to any of your children?

SALINGER: No.

CALLAGY: Have you ever conveyed any copyright interest to your wife?

SALINGER: No.

CALLAGY: Have you executed any sort of trust agreement which would during your lifetime convey any copyright interest to anyone else?

SALINGER: No.

CALLAGY: Does any individual, to your knowledge, have any financial or property interest in any of your literary works?

PAUL: I am going to object to the form of the question. Are you intending to include an agent, a percentage that might be due an agent, in that question?

CALLAGY: Aside from a literary agent who would be entitled to the customary 10 or 15 percent—

SALINGER: No.

CALLAGY: —does any other person have any financial or property interest in your work?

SALINGER: Foreign agents also receive a small percentage.

CALLAGY: Have you ever read any of Mr. Ian Hamilton's previously published work?

SALINGER: Read it through?

CALLAGY: Yes.

SALINGER: No.

CALLAGY: Have you read his biography on [Robert] Lowell, biography of Lowell?

SALINGER: I've looked at it.

CALLAGY: When did you do that?

SALINGER: It was on a stack at the bookstore.

CALLAGY: Do you recall when you looked at it?

SALINGER: No.

CALLAGY: Did you look at it prior to the time that you became aware that Mr. Hamilton was writing a biography of you?

SALINGER: I couldn't say. I don't know.

CALLAGY: Do you recall for what purpose you looked at it?

SALINGER: No, just walking through a bookstore and turning over pages.

CALLAGY: You have previously indicated that you first became aware of the existence of certain of your correspondence at the time you reviewed the May galleys to Mr. Hamilton's biography, is that correct?

SALINGER: Would you say that again?

[*Question read.*]

SALINGER: Sorry. It's just not clear. What do you mean by "certain correspondence"?

CALLAGY: Letters that you had written to third parties.

SALINGER: You mean to my son and to—or anything of that kind?

PAUL: No. That is not what Mr. Callagy means.

You testified before that the first time you became aware of the existence of the letters which are in the May galleys was when you read the May galleys, and Mr. Callagy just wants you to confirm whether or not that's what you said.

SALINGER: I believe so.

CALLAGY: Have you entered into any contracts with anyone respecting any correspondence which you may have written during your lifetime which is currently available?

SALINGER: No.

CALLAGY: Have you negotiated any licensing agreements for anyone to use any correspondence which you have written during your lifetime?

SALINGER: No.

CALLAGY: Do you have any plans to publish any of that correspondence?

SALINGER: No.

CALLAGY: Have you ever written to Harold Ober Associates regarding the possibility of publishing the letters that you wrote during your lifetime?

SALINGER: No.

CALLAGY: Do you intend to publish any letters that you wrote during your lifetime?

SALINGER: No.

PAUL: Wait a minute. Do you intend to publish them during your time or do you intend to publish letters you've written during your lifetime?

CALLAGY: Do you have current plans to publish any letters that you wrote during your lifetime?

SALINGER: No, I don't, no.

CALLAGY: Have you discussed with anyone the possibility that you might publish letters that you wrote during your lifetime?

SALINGER: No.

CALLAGY: Have you discussed with anyone the fact that you would not publish letters that you wrote during your lifetime?

SALINGER: No.

CALLAGY: Has your agent suggested to you that you might consider publishing letters that you have written?

SALINGER: No.

CALLAGY: Has anyone suggested to you that you might consider publishing letters that you have written?

SALINGER: No.

CALLAGY: Has anyone ever asked you for permission to quote from any of your letters?

SALINGER: No. Wait a second. I'm not sure of that. Somebody may have in the past, somebody doing a book about somebody else and I knew that principal person, but I can't recall offhand who or under what circumstances. I've been alive a long time and there have been a lot of people. That's all I know.

CALLAGY: In that instance, do you recall whether or not you gave permission to quote from your letters?

SALINGER: I can't recall that, no.

CALLAGY: So you don't recall whether you did or you didn't?

SALINGER: No.

CALLAGY: Are you aware that certain of your letters are deposited at various libraries in the United States?

SALINGER: Yes.

CALLAGY: When did you become aware of that for the first time?

SALINGER: Through the—I suppose I could say through the bibliography on Hamilton's galleys.

CALLAGY: Prior to the time you read the bibliography to Hamilton's galleys, were you unaware that any of your letters were deposited in libraries?

SALINGER: Yes.

CALLAGY: At the time you became aware that those letters were deposited in various libraries, did you yourself speak to anyone at these libraries regarding the subject?

SALINGER: No.

CALLAGY: Did you write to any of these libraries yourself?

SALINGER: No.

CALLAGY: Other than counsel, did you cause anyone else to write to these libraries?

SALINGER: No.

CALLAGY: Other than counsel, did you cause anyone else to call these libraries?

SALINGER: No.

CALLAGY: Did you call any of the individuals that may have caused the letters to be deposited with the libraries?

SALINGER: Did I what?

CALLAGY: Did you call or speak to any individuals who may have caused the letters to be deposited with the libraries?

SALINGER: No.

CALLAGY: Did you ask any of these libraries to return the letters to you?

SALINGER: No.

CALLAGY: Did you ask any of the libraries for the names of any people who may have had access to the letters?

SALINGER: I've had no contact with the libraries, no.

CALLAGY: Now, Mr. Salinger, what I am going to do is to question you about various of the letters that are in issue in this case, and what we can do is seal this portion because I will be marking each of the letters and then asking you certain questions about them.

SALINGER: What does "seal" mean?

PAUL: It means it's pursuant to the direction of the court. It doesn't become part of the public record, okay?

SALINGER: Yes.

PAUL: Is this a convenient point, Mr. Callagy, to take a quick break?

•

Despite the sealing of the rest of the transcript, some of Salinger's comments surfaced. He referred to the young man who had written these long-ago letters as "gauche," "callow," and "effusive." "I wish . . . you could read letters you wrote 46 years ago. It is very painful reading," he said. Asked how often the young Salinger wrote to friends, the old Salinger replied: "Apart from too often? I don't know."

A judge initially let the Hamilton biography go forward, but an appeal by Salinger was successful in blocking it. The U.S. Supreme Court declined to hear the case. Hamilton re-wrote his book to incorporate the legal case and his dimming enthusiasm for Salinger. *In Search of J. D. Salinger*, published in 1988, received tepid reviews and sold poorly. Hamilton's career never recovered. He died in 2001.

FIRST CODA

STANDING IN FOR SALINGER
CONFESSIONS OF J.D.'S ONE-TIME LETTER WRITER

BY JOANNA SMITH RAKOFF
BOOK MAGAZINE
SEPTEMBER/OCTOBER 2002

If you really want to hear about it, if you really want to understand how and why I spent a year of my precious life as Jerome
David Salinger (Jerry to his friends, J. D. to his fans), you'll
need to do some goddamned work. Picture, if you will, a map
of the Eastern seaboard. Halfway down the coast, you'll find
Winston-Salem, North Carolina, its air eternally tinged with
the sweet scent of tobacco. Somewhere within the city limits,
on a narrow street in Old Salem, perhaps, sits a four-bedroom
Victorian, recently renovated, surrounded by magnolias and
azaleas. In this house is a boy—a boy I do not know, have
never met, never will meet—and this is the person on whom
you must zoom in. Tonight he sits at the dark wooden desk
in his bedroom, still half-dressed in his rumpled school uni-
form—blue Oxford, gray flannel pants—attempting to write
a story for his English class. Though he looks rather like the
other boys at his school, he is most emphatically not like these
boys, boys who spend all their time thinking about football
and lacrosse and the SATs. He has just finished reading *The
Catcher in the Rye* for the third time. He is sixteen years old.

Now, trace your finger up the map and let it rest on New
York City, a place our boy from North Carolina has never

visited. Much of what he knows about the city he gleaned from *Catcher* and his other favorite novel, *The Great Gatsby.* He imagines smoky rooms, red-lipped Vassar girls drinking tumblers of whiskey in hotel bars, wisecracking taxi drivers. He cannot picture Brooklyn, particularly not a tiny apartment in a dilapidated back house—an apartment without heat, without a sink in the kitchen. The girl that lives in this apartment washes her dishes in the chipped, pink bathtub. She is not much older than the boy, six or seven years. She rouges her lips like a '40s film star, dons kilts and twinsets and loafers, and imagines herself, like Franny Glass, as "a languid, sophisticated type," even as she stoops over her bathtub, scrubbing pots in a tattered kimono. Each morning, she gets on the subway in her crummy neighborhood and emerges from it under the starry ceiling of Grand Central, a few blocks from the Madison Avenue office in which she works, an office virtually unchanged since the days in which Holden Caulfield roamed the city, trolling for a date.

Finally, you need to go to New Hampshire, where a tall, dark-eyed man meditates in the back room of his simple, wood-frame house. In his eighties now and mostly deaf, he thrives on routine: each morning, he rises, eats breakfast, kisses his wife goodbye, and heads to his study, where he meditates and, allegedly, writes. He is a Buddhist, a vegetarian, the son of a man who made his living processing meat. His wife, thirty years his junior, is a nurse at the local hospital. She enjoys weaving tapestries. He enjoys watching television. A satellite dish crowns the top of their farmhouse. Every five years or so, he visits New York, the city in which he was born and raised, the city he made intimate—and eccentrically romantic—for several generations of readers. He hates the city now, but he needs to come, needs to meet with his agent, make sure she's handling the business of his books in exactly the way he likes. He visits her office and they head out to lunch. He says hello to the low-voiced girl who assists his agent, the girl who fields his questions about royalties and contracts, repeating her answers three and four times on the days when he doesn't feel like using his special, amplified phone, bought for him by his wife. The girl has dark hair and wears a plaid wool skirt, red lipstick.

The man, you already know, is Jerome David Salinger.

The boy, we'll get to later.

The girl, of course, is me.

That day, some years ago, Salinger shook my hand with salty kindness, and I experienced an unparalleled surge of excitement—not because I was meeting the reclusive writer, but because I possessed a secret, a strange and goofy secret that, if disclosed to the surprisingly sweet old man who held my right hand in both of his, would perhaps lead to some kind of angry scene and, I supposed, the loss of my peculiar and beloved job. I had, you see, adopted Mr. Salinger's persona, in a small and harmless way.

During that year—1996, the Salinger Year—I was a newly minted Ph.D.-in-English drop-out, filled with my own sense of myself as a Young Intellectual, imagining my future as a latter-day Susan Sontag or Mary McCarthy. I drank at parties for New Important Books, and read long, labyrinthine novels by Thomas Pynchon, Martin Amis, John Dos Passos. I read William Faulkner, Jean Rhys, Joan Didion, and Jane Bowles—writers whose bleak, relentless styles stood in stark opposition to the insufferable cuteness of Salinger, a writer whose aggressively quirky view of the world had always slightly irked me. My parents owned his entire oeuvre.

At work, however, it was nothing but Salinger. Each day, I fielded phone calls from rabid fans, curious reporters, and the occasional clueless scholar ("Would Mr. Salinger be interested in delivering the commencement address at Bergen College?") And then one day, after I'd been at Harold Ober Associates for a month or two, one of the agents came over to my desk and dumped a pile of mail on it. These, he explained, were the Salinger letters. He had been holding them for me—letters that had collected over the past few months—until I acclimated to the job. It was my responsibility to answer them.

I looked at the envelopes. Many were addressed by hand or on obviously ancient typewriters, and quite a few came from overseas. The flimsy, pastel airmail stationery struck me as particularly suited to Salinger's fiercely nostalgic world. Opening the letters, I found variations on a theme: Holden Caulfield, the fans wrote, is the only character in literature who is truly like me. And you, Mr. Salinger, are surely the same person as Holden Caulfield. Thus, you and I should be friends. "I'd get one helluva kick outta you if you wrote back and told me I was a bastard!" enthused one writer. "My mother says you won't write back," wrote a young girl, "but I told her you would. I know you will, because you understand what it's like to be surrounded by phonies." Salinger, of course, would not write back.

Along with the letters, I was given a few crumbling, yellowed carbons copies of sample responses. Composed in the '60s, they possessed the starched formality of pre-email correspondence: Dear Miss So-and-So, Many thanks for your recent letter to J. D. Salinger. As you may know, Mr. Salinger does not wish to receive mail from his readers. Thus, we cannot pass your kind note on to him. We thank you for your interest in Mr. Salinger's books.

Over the days that followed, I dutifully responded, updating and personalizing the Ober boilerplate (changed the "Miss" to "Ms."; added the word "sorry" in a few places). As the weeks wore on, it became clear that Salinger fans were different from devotees of other authors. Their love for Salinger resembled a teen's slobbery obsession with her favorite pop star. They spanned all age groups, nationalities, classes, races, and sexualities. At least half of them made it very clear that they never write letters to authors and they knew Salinger probably wasn't going to get their letters and if by some weird chance he did, he wouldn't respond—but they still hoped, had a goddamn feeling, that maybe he would. Salinger fans were smart. They were misfits. And, for all their cynical posturing, what they loved about Holden was not just his smart-alecky whinging or his refusal to conform to the expectations of adults, but his hopeless, dewy-eyed naïveté, his utter idealism. If Holden were to write a letter to Salinger, he too would hope to hell that somehow, some way, that irascible hermit would write a goddamned letter back.

Holden Caulfield, in his red hunting cap, is the ultimate romantic.

And I, in my red lipstick, was not so different.

Across from my massive wooden desk stood a built-in bookcase filled with Salinger's books in their unadorned covers—no images, no author photos, as stipulated in his contract—each volume translated into every known language. Each day, as I typed letters for my boss, the straight spines of Salinger's works lurked in my peripheral vision. Whenever I glanced up or daydreamed or stretched, there they were, an unchanging screen. Inadvertently, I memorized their titles, began to see their characteristic fonts and colors (mustard yellow, dead crimson) on the backs of my eyelids as I fell asleep each night. *Seymour: An Introduction*, my mind would shoot out at me. *Nine Stories.*

Maybe, I thought, I should give Salinger another chance. Or, no, I didn't actually think such a thing, not in any straightforward way. For all my intellectual posturing, I was not a particularly reflective girl. Rather, I became prone to telling others—the people at the parties I went to each weekend—that they should really reread Salinger, for they would find that the stuff does indeed hold up, though I had no idea, hadn't done so myself, and they wouldn't believe the kinds of letters the guy gets from fans. "What kind of letters?" they would ask. "Tell us more."

And so I would tell them about the Japanese girl and her Hello Kitty stationery—she included two letters, one in Japanese and one in English, thinking perhaps Salinger knew Japanese, because he was so smart. I told them about the Swedish man, exactly the same age as Salinger, who read *Catcher* when it first came out and had re-read it every year since, and now, finally, had decided to write to Salinger. I told them about the crazy people who sent scrawled, scary letters on dirty scraps of paper—I called these people Holdens Gone Awry—the people who had never outgrown their adolescent anger. I imitated their strange imitations of Holdenspeak—their liberal use of 1940s adjectives ("How marvelous!") and pet names ("My crumb-bum, Steve, also adores *Franny and Zooey*"), their insistence of modifying every noun with helluva ("I bet everybody tells you this, but *The Catcher in the Rye* is one helluva book"). And I told them about the teenage girls who professed their love for Holden, a boy who, they felt, really understood girls.

What I didn't tell them, these acquaintances of mine, was what I wrote back.

One morning in late winter, a handwritten letter arrived, bubbly girlish script crowding three sheets of wrinkly pencil-smudged paper. The writer was a freshman who hated high school. She hated school, particularly English class, which she was failing (the only book she liked was, of course, *Catcher*). Her mother, she said, would kill her if she failed English, so she asked her teacher if she could do something to bring her grade up. "There is something you can do," the teacher told her. "Write a letter to J. D. Salinger and make it good enough that he'll write back. If he writes back, I'll give you an A."

"I really need this A," the girl wrote. "It will bring my GPA up. My mother is mad at me all the time now. I know you understand."

Of course she knew he would understand. This is a man who created a character who boasts of being "the most terrific liar you ever saw in your life." Would Holden miss the opportunity for a work-free A? Actually, he probably would; he cared about passing his classes at Pency about as much as Salinger cares about his fan mail. Or, for that matter, as much as Salinger himself cared about his own academic performance—like Holden, he failed out of numerous high schools.

I swiveled my chair toward my prehistoric IBM Selectric typewriter—Ober still hadn't entered the digital age—and pattered out a response to the girl, suggesting that it was decidedly not in the spirit of her hero to be worrying about grades or her mother's fury. If she wanted to be like Holden, she should accept her failing grade—a grade she, by her own admission, deserved—and tell her mother to go to hell. Would Salinger help out such a pathetic fool of a girl? No, he most certainly would not. By this point I had read and re-read his books—stayed late at work one night and slipped slim paperback editions into my tote bag—and I was certain I knew what Salinger would and would not say or do. I'd been surprised by how much I liked the work—it wasn't cutesy at all, I saw. In fact, it was dark, as dark and bleak as Jean Rhys, in certain ways. Franny Glass, pale and fainting in her sheared-raccoon coat, beating at the tired trappings of her life, struck a particular chord with me. Salinger liked girls who were honest, girls overcome with the world's thorniest questions, girls obsessed with saints and martyrs, genius girls like Franny. Not stupid little girls who couldn't even admit to their own failures. "If you desire an A—or, at the very least, a passing grade—there's only way to earn it," I typed, the Selectric humming in its satisfying, cat-like way. "You must study and do the work assigned to you. An A earned by trickery means absolutely nothing."

It should be clear by now that if there was a line to cross—the loosely sewn seam between bemused interest and freaky over-involvement—I had most certainly crossed it. Each morning, when the mail was dumped on my desk, I stopped whatever I was doing and ripped open the latest letters. While I mocked the Salinger fans, albeit gently, with my friends, when I was alone with their letters I felt a certain charge, a mixture of anger and love, disdain and empathy, admiration and disgust. You see, these people wrote to me—or to Salinger, care of me—about their lives, their social problems, their marital frustrations. It wasn't long before I was firing off consolation to the mother whose daughter, dead of some unmentionable disease at a young age, loved "A Perfect Day for Bananafish" and dreamed of writing a novel as an adult. I took to filching the fan letters, nervously stuffing them in my bag at the end of the day, not sure exactly what I would do with them, but certain they shouldn't be trashed, these documents of people's lives.

Salinger, I thought, would have done the same thing. And so would have Franny, Zooey, Seymour, and Holden, certainly they would have. Franny, clutching her little cloth copy of *The Way of the Pilgrim*, would cry over these letters, would keep them in her overcrowded purse, folding and unfolding them until they fell apart at the creases.

You are probably wondering, right about now, if I signed my own name to the letters I wrote to Salinger's fans—or if I actually pretended to be Salinger, signed a loopy "J. D." at the bottom of the page. It would be, perhaps, a better story had I done the latter, but, you see, I believed so utterly in the Salinger myth—in Salinger's right to be left utterly and completely alone—that I needed to write the letters as me, puffing with pleasure at my role as Salinger's gatekeeper, defender, and guardian angel, reminder of the Way of Salinger. It was, indeed, my own name that I used. Once a World War II veteran responded to my brief note, asking if I bore any relation to some other Rakoff whom he'd known in the service. This letter, shakily scratched on two sheets of plain white stationery with a leaking blue ballpoint pen, had me near tears. This man had written a letter to an author—an author who never, ever writes back—and instead found a girl, the daughter or granddaughter of his Army buddy, a connection to his past, to his *Catcher* days. I wanted, badly, to write back, to say, "Yes, that man is my father"—for it could have been, easily, in some fictional, pre-digital universe of coincidence and kismet, in Salinger's sepia-toned New York, where letters are a conduit to understanding, a key to discovery. I kept the letter until I found a moment to call my dad and ask him if he knew the man mentioned, the other Rakoff. He didn't.

And so I didn't write back, just as I didn't write a second time to the schoolgirl seeking an easy A, who responded to my note with expletives, angry that I wouldn't pass on her letter to Salinger, and even angrier that I had taken her to task for her efforts. Who was I to judge her, she asked. Did I know what it was like to be a teenage girl? She wondered if I had ever been young, or was simply a dried up spinster with nothing better to do than berate strangers and meddle in their business, much like her English teacher. I began to wonder the same thing, or something like it. Was my life so wonderful that I could advise or console this girl and others like her?

For the Salinger fans, books were not texts to be taken apart, as I was taught in my Ph.D. program, nor were they springboards for progressive thought, as I was taught in college, nor attempts to rip apart language, to challenge the reader's bourgeois sense of comfort, as my boyfriend and his friends kept saying. No, for the Salinger fans, books were simply worlds to inhabit—sad and electric worlds in which smart, funny, disappointed people discuss ideas and smoke cigarettes and speak their minds. His stories don't possess the kind of arc we associate with great narratives. There are no marriage plots or conspiracy plots or even sex plots; there is no real suspense. Instead, Salinger simply gives us people—heightened, hypersensitive versions of ourselves—who think too much, people in the midst of existential crises, people who cannot—like Holden and Franny and Seymour—bear the conventions of contemporary society. They have not made the transition from childhood to adulthood, these characters; they resist the expectations placed on them, the roles they must play as bona fide grown-ups. Salinger Land—much like Disneyland or Never Never Land—is a place in which the trappings of adulthood are something to be feared. The only proper response to such terror is to take to one's couch, weeping into a little book, or to have a nervous breakdown, or to kill oneself.

Alternatively, one could hide out in a dark office, writing letters to complete strangers.

Or one could publish a number of books, then simply refuse to have any further contact with the world.

Or one could obsess over a reclusive author. One could begin to regard the characters created by this author as real people. One could adopt their speech patterns and mannerisms and trademark red caps.

Or, to look at it another way, one could—if one happens to be a boy from North Carolina—sit in one's room, reading and re-reading *Catcher*, much as the novel's hero sits in his dorm room, reading Isak Dinesen and Thomas Hardy. "What really knocks me out," Holden explains, "is a book that, when you're all done reading it, you wish the author that wrote it was a terrific friend of yours and you could call him up on the phone whenever you felt like it." And this, my friends, is what we call irony.

Half a century ago, Salinger, the future recluse, perfectly expressed that nebulous feeling that any real reader feels after finishing a terrific book: you want the characters to stay with you, to appear at the foot of your bed, ready to further discuss their plights. But in giving shape to this sentiment he essentially invited his readers to call him up on the phone whenever they felt like it. Like the letters from Salinger fans, Holden dares you to engage him in a dialogue. *The Catcher in the Rye* is a love letter, a love letter and a suicide note, and its author begs you—goddamn pleads with you—to write him back, to insert yourself into the narrative. But for Salinger, the narrative has changed.

And what about that boy in North Carolina? It is late now. He puts down his paperback copy of *Catcher*. The crimson has worn away from the cover's edges. He sits down at his new computer and types "Dear Mr. Salinger." He explains that he's just finished *Catcher* for the third time, that the book is a masterpiece, that most of what he reads bores him, most writers are utterly insincere.

"I think about Holden a lot," he writes. "He just pops into my mind's eye and I get to thinking about him dancing with old Phoebe or horsing around in front of the bathroom mirror at Pencey. When I first think about him I usually get a big stupid grin on my face. You know, thinking about what a funny guy he is and all. But then, I usually get depressed as hell. I guess I get depressed because I only think about Holden when I'm feeling very emotional. I can get quite emotional. Don't worry, though. I've learned that, as phony as it may be, you can't go around revealing your goddamn emotions to the world."

No, you can't simply bleed all over the world—at least, not after puberty hits. The Boy from North Carolina was right. But you *can* write a letter to J. D. Salinger, explaining your thoughts on love and books, you can have the weird confidence to picture Salinger—looking as he does in his most famous photo, black hair and blacker eyes, eager grin—reading your letter and smiling to read your description of *Catcher* as a masterpiece, thrilling to find you agree with him about *Gatsby* ("What a determined sonuvabitch! I really liked him") and girls ("I used to get nervous as hell around them, especially the really good-looking ones"), to find that—what a coincidence!—you express yourself in much the same way as Holden Caulfield.

When the real, actual J. D. Salinger—with his thin grey hair and saucer-sized ears and same kind, self-deprecating smile—visited our office, I shook his hand (or, really, he shook mine), said "nice to meet you," smoothed my skirt and turned back to my typing. In my desk lay the letter from North Carolina, two neatly typed pages, unfurled from a laser printer, and ending:

> I'll write you again soon. I can hardly wait. Anyway, my line of thought is this: If I was the guy who put myself onto paper and I came out in the form of *The Catcher in the Rye*, I'd get a bang out of the bastard who had the nerve to write me a letter pretending (and wanting) to be able to do the same thing.

As the door to my boss's smoke-clogged office closed, a thought slashed through my brain—What if I gave Salinger the letter? Wouldn't he be, at the very least, amused by it? With my left hand, I slid open the cold metal drawer, fingered the slightly worn white sheets—I'd read it several times, unsure of how to respond. Should I write back and tell him what a kick the letter had given me? Should I tell him he could certainly do what Salinger did—write a groundbreaking, beloved book—if he simply applied himself?

When I went to lunch, I slipped the note into the pocket of my coat and read it again while standing in line to buy my salad. Three hours later, my boss returned to the office alone. I read the letter again, wondering if Salinger would come back to finish up some business. He didn't, of course. And neither did he—or my boss—ever find out about my personal responses to the Salinger letters, to all the Salinger letters except one. I never wrote back to the boy from North Carolina. Instead, I kept the letter, occasionally rereading it, wondering if he ever wrote again to Salinger. I didn't stick around to find out. After a year, I left Ober to become a writer myself. Each season I scan the publishers' catalogues, looking to see if that boy ever wrote that novel. This would be a better story, wouldn't it, if he had?

That's all I'm going to tell about. I could probably tell you about what happened to me after I left Ober—that I exchanged my sad lodgings for a nice one-bedroom with a big double sink. A lot of people, though, especially my old friends who wondered what was going on with me during that year, the Salinger Year, why I was so quiet and thin and strange, still ask me about the Salinger letters, what they mean to me and the world, and do I think people still write them? Do the people who have had my job since I left, the parade of bohemian youths willing to work for nearly nothing in order to be around literature, answer them the way I did? Holden would say those are stupid questions. How do you know what anything really means? Or what anyone else might do in any given situation? If you want to know the truth, I don't know what I think about it. In certain ways, I'm sorry I've told so many people about the Salinger fans, sorry to have made fun of them at cocktail parties, sorry not to have kept their love private, between the typewriter and myself. About all I know is—and, again, maybe you've guessed this; I've already told you I'm not a girl who's prone to reflection—about all I know is, I sort of miss them.

BETRAYING SALINGER

I SCORED THE PUBLISHING COUP OF THE DECADE: HIS FINAL BOOK. AND THEN I BLEW IT.

BY ROGER LATHBURY
NEW YORK MAGAZINE
APRIL 4, 2010

The first letter I got from J. D. Salinger was very short. It was 1988, and I had written to him with a proposal: I wanted my tiny publishing house, Orchises Press, to publish his novella *Hapworth 16, 1924*. And Salinger himself had improbably replied, saying that he would consider it.

Hapworth is Salinger's great mystical not-quite-lost work. It takes the form of a digressive 26,000-word letter sent home from summer camp by the breathtakingly precocious 7-year-old Seymour Glass. The novella took up more than 50 pages of *The New Yorker* in the issue of June 19, 1965; I was 18 then, and I still have my copy. It's the last writing that Salinger released to the world, apart from court documents blocking assaults on his privacy, and it never appeared again.

I had the idea that Salinger might find my company attractive for its smallness. (Orchises is based in Alexandria, Virginia, and at the time had about 50 titles in print, mostly poetry and reprints of classics.) I had addressed my pitch to "J. D. Salinger, Cornish, NH," figuring that the post office would know what to do. They did. Two weeks later, a short note arrived, signed "J D S," and saying that he'd consider my proposal. I was ecstatic, even if I doubted that he'd proceed. And then, silence.

Eight years went by. In 1996, Harold Ober Associates, which represented Salinger, asked for a catalogue and some sample books. It had been so long, I didn't make any connection, but I now see that I was being vetted. That May, I came home from vacation to find a letter from Phyllis Westberg, Harold Ober's president. She began, "It might be wiser to sit down before reading the rest of this . . ."

She summarized my communication with Mr. Salinger and said that he would soon write to me. I phoned her, in shock, just to be sure. Westberg warned me that the book would have to be made to exacting standards. (I remember thinking, *That means F cloth*—the highest grade of buckram bookbinding fabric.)

Why had he said yes? I think he chose me because I didn't chase him. I had left him alone for eight years after receiving his letter; I wasn't pushy in the commercial way he found offensive.

Two weeks later, a large envelope arrived. It had been addressed on a Royal manual typewriter, the same as the 1988 note. Inside was a full-page letter, and it took my breath away. Chatty, personal, with that rare sweet and endearing tone that characterizes the story I wanted to publish, it expressed Salinger's high pleasure in finding a way to put out *Hapworth*. He proposed a meeting. Just by chance (Could this be true?), he would soon be close to Washington, D.C. Might we have lunch?

Later that week, I was in my office and the phone rang. "Mr. Lathbury, please." "That's me." "This is Salinger." I swallowed. "I, um, am glad you called. Thank you for your letter."

Then J. D. Salinger pitched me his story, like an unknown, saying that he thought it was a high point of his writing. "I don't know how I managed to finish it." Some instinct told me not to offer praise, which would have been superfluous. (Hadn't I wanted to publish the story?) He proposed a lunch at the National Gallery of Art. Shaking with astonishment, I set up a time the following Wednesday.

That week, I typed out the text of "Hapworth 16, 1924" from my old *New Yorker*, and designed a dummy that I thought would meet Salinger's demands. I gave the story plenty of leading (the space between lines of type) so that, as Salinger had put it, "Seymour could breathe." That bulked up the book, solving another problem. Salinger had told me that he strongly preferred type on a book's spine to read horizontally rather than vertically, and the volume had been too slim for that.

As I worked out the specifications, I tried deliberately not to make the book "elegant." He had been quick to object to my use of the word, which to him connoted narcissism and preciousness. The buckram he asked me to use is the functional, unpretty material that libraries use to rebind worn-out books. *Hapworth*, the book, was to start out this way: straightforward and pure.

When I arrived at the National Gallery, Salinger—tall, in good shape at 77, with silver hair and a blue kerchief around his neck—was waiting. We shook hands, proceeded through the cafeteria lines, and found a table in the middle of the room. Just two guys discussing papers pulled from an old briefcase. He was losing his hearing and was slightly embarrassed about it, but if I leaned in and spoke a little louder than normal, he could manage. Salinger disconcertingly asked me to call him "Jerry." I was nervous, though small talk came easily enough. Surprisingly, he touched on matters about which I would never have dared inquire, such as his resentment over the lawyers' fees in his suit against biographer Ian Hamilton. He also made the disparaging remark that he found Little, Brown, his publisher since 1951, completely unsympathetic. I resolved that he wouldn't find Orchises so. Still, when I said, "Shall we get down to business?" he too relaxed perceptibly.

I had prepared two typographical treatments for the text, and he chose the one I thought he would. We went over small details of bookmaking. (Running heads at the top of the page? No. The fabric headband at the ends of the spine? Plain navy blue. "Can't go wrong with that!" Salinger said, with an explosive laugh.) The cover would carry just the title and, below it, his name. There would be no dust jacket. I showed him a mock-up of the spine, and when he saw the horizontal type, he said, warmly, "Oh good."

I confessed that my distribution wasn't great. He told me, "Nothing would make me happier than not to see my book in the Dartmouth Bookstore." Distributed but not distributed! Of all the writers I have published, only one has ever asked that his book be kept out of stores.

I had spotted a few inconsistencies within the text, and I brought them up, fearing the wrath of the lion. Yet he said, mildly enough, "No, no. I want it left as it is." He reminisced about reading *The New Yorker* page proofs in the car of his editor, William Shawn, while Shawn attended an event at his son's prep school.

What would be the publication date? This I had ready: "January 1, 1997." Six months off.

"That's my birthday."

"I think I knew that." In fact, I had chosen it for that reason.

We wrapped up a few details, and bussed our trays. I stopped to stare at the waterfall outside the cafeteria, which flows over a set of stone steps right up against a glass wall. Suddenly, Salinger wheeled around. "What are you looking at? Answer quick, without thinking!"

Taken aback, I stammered, "I like that waterfall." He seemed mollified. In a moment I understood: Had I paused so he could be secretly photographed? A friend later told me that such pictures can be sold for large sums.

Money, though, was not on my mind, nor on his. There was never talk of an advance, and although he did not want the book aggressively priced, he had told his agent, generously, to let me make some money on it. I worked out that I could sell the book for $15.95.

After refusing my offer of a ride, J. D. Salinger walked energetically across the Mall. I was both relieved and sad to see him go, and wondered if this would be the only time we would meet.

A series of letters followed. They were remarkably open, even garrulous, with notes on family life, social observations, gripes about train travel, little jokes about himself. He mentioned working on Glass-family stories, but told me nothing about what he'd written after *Hapworth*. I certainly didn't ask.

Around this time, I unwittingly made the first move that would unravel the whole deal. I applied for Library of Congress Cataloging in Publication data.

It sounds innocent. It is certainly boring. CIP data are the information printed on the copyright page. The filings are public information, but I didn't imagine that anyone would notice one among thousands. It would be like reading a list of register codes at the grocery: apples 30, bananas 45, oranges 61.

As we worked on the book, the publication date slipped from January to February. An agreement was drawn up, saying that *Hapworth* had to appear by June 1, or the deal would expire. There was also an unusual provision: All copies were to be sold at the retail price, whether to individuals or distributors or bookstores. Salinger would get his wish of limited distribution. What store would sell a book on which it could make nothing?

One thing Salinger did tell me was that he'd grown unhappy about seeing his name on the front cover, and we removed it. This was going to be a most austere book. We also learned that the type on the spine was too small to be stamped cleanly into the fabric. Salinger offered a new design, with the letters strung out diagonally. It was awful: ugly, difficult to read, ostentatiously weird. When I said so to Phyllis Westberg, she was succinct: "Bite the bullet, Roger!"

I bit. I ordered two sample cases—the covers of the book, its shell. In November, I sent one to Cornish, and kept the other. We would have *Hapworth* in stores in just a few weeks.

Then I made another, bigger mistake.

What I know now, but did not then, was that CIP

listings are not only public but also appear on Amazon.com, even for books not yet published. Someone spotted *Hapworth* there, and his sister was a reporter for a local paper in Arlington, the *Washington Business Journal.* One day, after I arrived home from my job teaching at George Mason University, she telephoned.

It seems clear now how everything happened. Hindsight is always clear. I remember that the reporter told me this would be an article about Orchises Press as well as Salinger. She asked me basic questions, about how I'd got Salinger to say yes, about the size of the press run. Foolishly—if reasonably—I answered most of them. I compared our press run to those of Salinger's earlier books, mentioning them by name. I thought I could control myself, but my ego came into play. Anyway, what harm could it do? This was a tiny paper.

Then someone at *The Washington Post* saw it. A writer, David Streitfeld, called. I refused to speak at first, then answered a few questions, nervously, about what I liked about *Hapworth* and when it would appear. He asked if I'd met Salinger, and that, at least, I kept to myself.

The story appeared in the *Post* in January 1997. My phone nearly exploded. Newspapers, magazines, television stations, book distributors, strangers, foreign publishers, movie people. South Africa, Catalonia, Australia. The fax machine ran through reams of paper. People wanting review copies. (There were to be none.) People wanting interviews. I held as closely as I could to "No comment," but when asked for a publication date, I gave one—at first March 1997, then later. I held to the $15.95 price for everybody: bookstore, distributor, chain store, fruit stand, anyone who wanted *Hapworth.*

The only one who didn't call me was Salinger. I asked his agent, and repeatedly got the same answer: No news. I couldn't proceed without him, because we still had too many details unsettled.

Meanwhile, bookstore chains—frustrated by the no-discount rule—had decided to simply mark the book up to $22.95. I inferred (from Westberg's questions) that Salinger thought I had jacked up the price to capitalize on the publicity and gouge everyone. I hadn't, but I'll never know for sure what he believed.

By February 1997, I had heard nothing for three months, but I had not yet given up hope. On February 20, Michiko Kakutani, working from the original text in *The New Yorker*, published a punishing review of *Hapworth* in *The New York Times*. I have no way of knowing, but this may have been the last straw. It was as rough as anything that Mary McCarthy or any other critic had ever said about Salinger's work.

I yearned to write to Salinger, but I knew that it would do no good. He must have been furious with me for betraying him by leaking news to the press, or even confirming it. I could no longer be trusted. I had proven myself part of the crass, opportunistic world that Salinger's heroes disdain.

We were at a standoff, and soon enough, the contract's time limit passed. I lost the book on June 1. Westberg's office told me then that any subsequent moves would be up to Salinger, and that was that.

Some people, when they hear this story, blame Salinger for backing down after going this far, but I find this unfair. Such people want J. D. Salinger to be someone other than J. D. Salinger. Nor is the problem *The Washington Post*. I know where the blame lies. After thinking I could do right by a man I admired, I let him down.

In the end, I'm left with a box. It contains the buckram sample case and the die used to stamp the cockeyed spine printing. It also contains a stack of wonderful, kind letters from a man who has meant as much to readers as any writer ever can. I have not looked at those letters in years; to reread them would be too painful. Nor will I sell them. That, at least, I can do.

J. D. SALINGER (b. 1919, New York, NY; d. 2010, Cornish, NH) was one of the most influential writers of the twentieth century. His landmark novel *The Catcher in the Rye* is widely established as a defining novel of post–World War II America. He is also the author of *Nine Stories, Franny and Zooey*, and *Raise High the Roof Beam, Carpenters*, and *Seymour: An Introduction*. Though he continued to write up until his death in 2010, Salinger was fiercely reclusive and stopped publishing his work in 1965.

DAVID STREITFELD is a Pulitzer Prize–winning journalist who writes for *The New York Times*. He was the editor of *Gabriel García Márquez: The Last Interview* and *Philip K. Dick: The Last Interview*.

WILLIAM MAXWELL was a long-time fiction editor at *The New Yorker*, as well as the author of several novels, including the classic *So Long, See You Tomorrow*. He died in 2000.

SHIRLIE BLANEY was a high school student when she got to know Salinger. She has not spoken about the experience for many years.

LACEY FOSBURGH was a *New York Times* reporter. She covered Salinger's lawsuit against numerous bookstores for selling a pirated collection of his stories. When she called his agent and asked for an interview, Salinger called her back that day. Fosburgh died in 1993.

GREG HERRIGES has written seven novels, a collection of short stories, and *JD: A Memoir of a Time and a Journey*, about his encounter with Salinger. He won Aurora Awards for documentary screenwriting and producing for *TC Boyle: The Art of the Story* and *Player: A Rock and Roll Dream*. A professor of English at William Rainey Harper College, he lives in Deerfield, Illinois.

MICHAEL CLARKSON is the author of eight nonfiction books, including *Intelligent Fear* and *The Age of Daredevils*. He gives presentations to organizations on fear and stress. He lives in Fort Erie, Ontario, with his wife, Jennifer.

BETTY EPPES was a longtime Baton Rouge journalist. She is now retired.

JOANNA SMITH RAKOFF is the author of the memoir *My Salinger Year*, an international bestseller and finalist for *Elle*'s 2014 Grand Prix des Lectrices, and the novel *A Fortunate Age*, winner of the Goldberg Prize for Jewish Fiction and the *Elle* Readers' Prize. She writes for *The New York Times*, *Vogue*, and many other publications.

ROGER LATHBURY is a professor of English at George Mason University in Fairfax, Virginia, where he teaches American literature, modern British poetry, and nonsense prose and poetry. Since 1983, he has operated Orchises Press, which specializes in poetry, reprints (some of them facsimiles of rare editions), and other selected titles, of which *Hapworth 16, 1924* was to be one. He and his wife live in Alexandria and have two daughters.

THE LAST INTERVIEW SERIES

KURT VONNEGUT: THE LAST INTERVIEW

"I think it can be tremendously refreshing if a creator of literature has something on his mind other than the history of literature so far. Literature should not disappear up its own asshole, so to speak."

$15.95 / $17.95 CAN
978-1-61219-090-7
ebook: 978-1-61219-091-4

LEARNING TO LIVE FINALLY: THE LAST INTERVIEW
JACQUES DERRIDA

"I am at war with myself, it's true, you couldn't possibly know to what extent . . . I say contradictory things that are, we might say, in real tension; they are what construct me, make me live, and will make me die."

translated by PASCAL-ANNE BRAULT and MICHAEL NAAS
$15.95 / $17.95 CAN
978-1-61219-094-5
ebook: 978-1-61219-032-7

ROBERTO BOLAÑO: THE LAST INTERVIEW

"Posthumous: It sounds like the name of a Roman gladiator, an unconquered gladiator. At least that's what poor Posthumous would like to believe. It gives him courage."

translated by SYBIL PEREZ and others
$15.95 / $17.95 CAN
978-1-61219-095-2
ebook: 978-1-61219-033-4

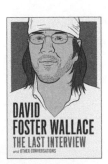

DAVID FOSTER WALLACE: THE LAST INTERVIEW

"I don't know what you're thinking or what it's like inside you and you don't know what it's like inside me. In fiction. . . we can leap over that wall itself in a certain way."

$15.95 / $15.95 CAN
978-1-61219-206-2
ebook: 978-1-61219-207-9

THE LAST INTERVIEW SERIES

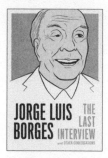

JORGE LUIS BORGES: THE LAST INTERVIEW

"Believe me: the benefits of blindness have been greatly exaggerated. If I could see, I would never leave the house, I'd stay indoors reading the many books that surround me."

translated by KIT MAUDE

$15.95 / $15.95 CAN
978-1-61219-204-8
ebook: 978-1-61219-205-5

HANNAH ARENDT: THE LAST INTERVIEW

"There are no dangerous thoughts for the simple reason that thinking itself is such a dangerous enterprise."

$15.95 / $15.95 CAN
978-1-61219-311-3
ebook: 978-1-61219-312-0

RAY BRADBURY: THE LAST INTERVIEW

"You don't have to destroy books to destroy a culture. Just get people to stop reading them."

$15.95 / $15.95 CAN
978-1-61219-421-9
ebook: 978-1-61219-422-6

JAMES BALDWIN: THE LAST INTERVIEW

"You don't realize that you're intelligent until it gets you into trouble."

$15.95 / $15.95 CAN
978-1-61219-400-4
ebook: 978-1-61219-401-1

THE LAST INTERVIEW SERIES

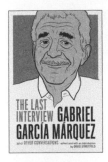

GABRIEL GÁRCIA MÁRQUEZ: THE LAST INTERVIEW

"The only thing the Nobel Prize is good for is not having to wait in line."

$15.95 / $15.95 CAN
978-1-61219-480-6
ebook: 978-1-61219-481-3

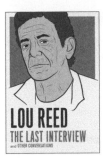

LOU REED: THE LAST INTERVIEW

"Hubert Selby. William Burroughs. Allen Ginsberg. Delmore Schwartz . . . I thought if you could do what those writers did and put it to drums and guitar, you'd have the greatest thing on earth."

$15.95 / $15.95 CAN
978-1-61219-478-3
ebook: 978-1-61219-479-0

ERNEST HEMINGWAY: THE LAST INTERVIEW

"The most essential gift for a good writer is a built-in, shockproof, shit detector."

$15.95 / $20.95 CAN
978-1-61219-522-3
ebook: 978-1-61219-523-0

PHILIP K. DICK: THE LAST INTERVIEW

"The basic thing is, how frightened are you of chaos? And how happy are you with order?"

$15.95 / $20.95 CAN
978-1-61219-526-1
ebook: 978-1-61219-527-8

THE LAST INTERVIEW SERIES

NORA EPHRON: THE LAST INTERVIEW

"You better *make* them care about what you think. It had better be quirky or perverse or thoughtful enough so that you hit some chord in them. Otherwise, it doesn't work."

$15.95 / $20.95 CAN
978-1-61219-524-7
ebook: 978-1-61219-525-4

JANE JACOBS: THE LAST INTERVIEW

"I would like it to be understood that all our human economic achievements have been done by ordinary people, not by exceptionally educated people, or by elites, or by supernatural forces."

$15.95 / $20.95 CAN
978-1-61219-534-6
ebook: 978-1-61219-535-3

AUG - - 2017